15 –MINUTE
ARABIC
LEARN IN JUST 12 WEEKS

MARION SARHAAN

Senior Editors Angeles Gavira, Christine Stroyan
Project Art Editor Vanessa Marr
Jacket Design Development Manager Sophia MTT
Jacket Designer Juhi Sheth
Pre-Producer David Almond
Senior Producer Ana Vallarino
Publisher Liz Wheeler
Publishing Director Jonathan Metcalf

Language content for Dorling Kindersley by
g-and-w publishing.

First American Edition, 2009
This revised edition published in the United States in 2018
by DK Publishing, 345 Hudson Street,
New York, New York 10014

18 19 20 21 22   10 9 8 7 6 5 4 3 2 1
001–305458–Apr/2018

Published in Great Britain by Dorling Kindersley Limited.

A catalog record for this book is available from the
Library of Congress.
ISBN 978-1-4654-6293-0

DK books are available at special discounts when
purchased in bulk for sales promotions, premiums, fund-
raising, or educational use. For details, contact DK
Publishing Special Markets, 345 Hudson Street, New
York, New York 10014 or SpecialSales@dk.com

Printed in China

A WORLD OF IDEAS:
SEE ALL THERE IS TO KNOW

www.dk.com

CONTENTS

How to use this book

This book teaches the Egyptian spoken dialect of Arabic (see page 9). The main part of the book is devoted to 12 themed chapters, broken down into five 15-minute daily lessons, the last of which is a refersher lesson. So, in just 12 weeks you will have completed the course. A concluding reference section contains a menu guide, an English-to-Arabic dictionary, and a guide to the Arabic script.

18   WEEK 2

Warm up (1 minute)

Count to ten. (pp.10–11)

Remind yourself how to say "hello" and "goodbye." (pp.8–9)

Ask "Do you (plural) have any children?" (pp.14–15)

Fil kafiterya
In the coffee house

The traditional Arab café (**il-ahwa**), in the [...] male-oriented, offers Arabic coffee or blac[...] (water or "hubble bubble") pipes, and perh[...] of backgammon or dominoes. In recent tim[...] coffee houses have sprung up, catering to [...] all ages and genders.

Words to remember (5 minutes)

Familiarize yourself with these phrases.

شاي بحليب	tea with milk
shay bi-нaleeb	
شاي بنعناع	mint tea
shay bi-naanaaa	
سندويتش	sandwich
sandawitsh	
توست ومربى	toast and jam
tost wi murabba	

ة بدون حليب
ahwa bidoon н[...]
black coffee

Warm up

Each day starts with a warm up that encourages you to recall vocabulary or phrases you have learned previously. To the right of the heading bar you will see how long you need to spend on each exercise.

Instructions

Each exercise is numbered and introduced by instructions that explain what to do. In some cases additional information is given about the language point being covered.

Cultural tip Traditional Arabic coffee is served in a smal[...] cup, and is black and very strong. Brewed in a special jug, it [...] comes in three basic styles: **saada** (without sugar); **mazboot** (medium sweet); and **ziyaada** (very sweet).

Cultural/Conversational tip

These panels provide additional insights into life in the Arabic-speaking world and language usage.

In conversation (4 minutes)

آخذ شاي بدون حليب.
aakhud ahwa bi-нaleeb min faplak
I'll have a coffee with milk, please.

حاجة ثانية؟
нaaga tanya
Anything else?

دكم بسبوسة؟
aandukum bas[...]
Do you have [...] [semolina cak[...]

How to use the flap

The book's cover flaps allow you to conceal the Arabic so that you can test whether you have remembered correctly.

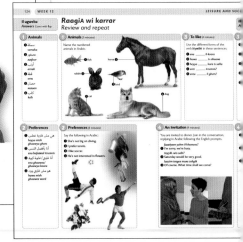

124   WEEK 12   LEISURE AND SOC[...]

il-agweba
Answers (Cover with flap)

RaagiA wi karrar
Review and repeat

1 Animals

1 سمكة *samaka*
2 حصور *нaṣoor*
3 أرنب *arnab*
4 قطة *otta*
5 حصان *нesaan*
6 كلب *kelb*

Animals (3 minutes)

Name the numbered animals in Arabic.

fish 1   horse 2
rabbit 3
5 bird
4 cat   6 dog

3 To like (4 minutes)

Use the different forms of the verb **biyнibb** in these sentences.
1 ena .... il-koora
2 howa .... is-sbaaнa
3 heyya .... kura lu safla
4 enti .... il-tennis?
5 enta .... il-ghani?

2 Preferences

1 هي مش ماولة غطس *heyya mish ghaweya ghars*
2 أنا أفضل التنس *ena bafaddal it-tennis*
3 أنا ماوي كودا *ena ghaweya/ ghaweya koora*
4 هو مش ماوي ورد *howa mish ghaweya ward*

Preferences (4 minutes)

Say the following in Arabic:
1 She's not big on diving.
2 I prefer tennis.
3 I like soccer.
4 He's not interested in flowers.

An invitation (4 minutes)

You are invited to dinner. Join in the conversation, replying in Arabic following the English prompts.
Aaatayyam john il khamees?
1 I'm sorry, we're busy.
Aayyib. wis-sabt?
2 Saturday would be very good.
laazim taagoo maaa zahgib
3 Of course. What time shall we come?

Revision pages

A recap of selected elements of previous lessons helps to reinforce your knowledge.

تورتة
torta
cake

سُكَّر
sukkar
sugar

قهوة بحليب
ahwa bi-Haleeb
coffee with milk

4 Useful phrases (5 minutes)

Learn these phrases. Read the English under the pictures and say the phrase in Arabic as shown on the right. Then cover the Arabic with the flap and test yourself.

آخذ شاي بدون حليب.
aakhud shay bidoon Haleeb

I'll have a black tea.

حاجة ثانية؟
Haaga tanya

Anything else?

عندكم فول؟
Aandukum fool

Do you have mashed fava beans?

كام الحساب؟
kaam il-Hisaab

How much is the bill?

Useful phrases
Selected phrases relevant to the topic help you speak and understand.

Read it
These panels explain how the Arabic script works, give tips for reading it, and show useful signs.

Read it The sign below reads *maтaar* (airport). It is written (from right to left): م (*m*), ط (*т*), ا (*aa*), ر (*r*). Notice that the first *a* is not written (see page 25 for more details on vowels in Arabic script).

مطار

أيوه، عندنا.
aywah. Aandina
Yes, we do.

شكرا. كام الحساب
من فضلك؟
shukran. kaam il-Hisaab min faвlak
Thank you. How much is the bill, please?

تسعة جنيه، من فضلك.
tisAa ginayh, min faвlak
Nine pounds, please.

Text styles
Distinctive text styles differentiate Arabic and English, and the pronunciation guide.

In conversation
Illustrated dialogs reflecting how vocabulary and phrases are used in everyday situations appear throughout the book.

Say it
In these exercises you are asked to apply what you have learned, using different vocabulary.

5 Say it (2 minutes)

Do you have a single room, please?

Six nights.

Is dinner included?

Dictionary
A mini-dictionary provides
ready reference from English
to Arabic for 2,500 words.

Menu guide
Use this guide as
a reference
for identifying
popular
Arabic dishes.

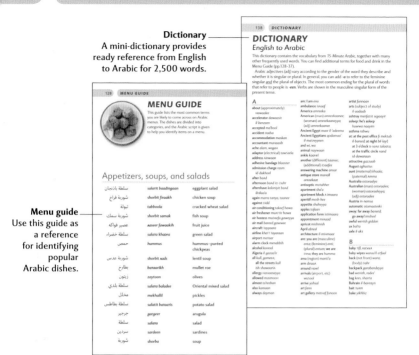

138   DICTIONARY

DICTIONARY
English to Arabic

This dictionary contains the vocabulary from 15-Minute Arabic, together with many other frequently used words. You can find additional terms for food and drink in the Menu Guide (pp.128–37).

Arabic adjectives (adj) vary according to the gender of the word they describe and whether it is singular or plural. In general, to add -a to refer to the feminine singular and the plural of objects. The most common ending for the plural of words that refer to people is -een. Verbs are shown in the masculine singular form of the present tense.

128   MENU GUIDE

MENU GUIDE

This guide lists the most common terms you are likely to come across on Arabic menus. The dishes are divided into categories, and the Arabic script is given to help you identify items on a menu.

Appetizers, soups, and salads

سلطة باذنجان	salatit baadingaan	eggplant salad
شوربة فراخ	shorbit firaakh	chicken soup
تبولة	tabboola	cracked wheat salad
شوربة سمك	shorbit samak	fish soup
عصير فواكه	aaseer fawaakih	fruit juice
سلطة خضراء	salata khaḍra	green salad
حمص	hummus	hummus—puréed chickpeas
شوربة عدس	shorbit aads	lentil soup
بطارخ	baṭaarikh	mullet roe
زيتون	zaytoon	olives
سلطة بلدي	salata baladee	Oriental mixed salad
مخلل	mekhallil	pickles
سلطة بطاطس	salatit baṭaaṭis	potato salad
جرجير	gargeer	arugula
سلطة	salaṭa	salad
سردين	sardeen	sardines
شوربة	shorba	soup

Pronunciation guide

Many of the sounds in Arabic are similar to their English equivalents, but some, indicated in this book by special characters, have no English equivalent:

h/H Arabic has two **h** sounds: **h** as in *horse*, and a second sound (**H**), as if breathing on glasses to clean them.

s/S There are two **s** sounds: **s** as in *silly*, and **S**, which is more voiced.

d/D There are two **d** sounds: **d** as in *ditch*, and **D**, which is more voiced.

t/T There are two **t** sounds: **t** as in *titch*, and **T**, which is more voiced.

z/Z There are two **z** sounds: **z** as in *zebra*, and **Z**, which is more voiced.

kh A throaty **h** pronounced as in the Scottish *loch*.

gh A sound produced as if pronouncing **r** from the back of the throat, rather than by rolling the tongue.

' A short pause or glottal stop as when the **tt** in *bottle* is dropped.

A A uniquely Arabic guttural sound similar to the exclamation *ah!*

Pronouncing these sounds correctly becomes easier the more you listen to spoken Arabic.

How to use the audio app

All the numbered exercises in each lesson, apart from the Warm ups at the beginning and the Say it exercises at the end, have recorded audio, available via a free app. The app also includes a function to record yourself and listen to yourself alongside native speakers.

To start using the audio with the book, first download the **DK 15 Minute Language Course** app on your smartphone or tablet from the App Store or Google Play. Open the app and scan the QR code on the back of this book to add it to your Library. As soon as the QR code is recognized, the audio will download.

There are two ways in which you can use the audio. The first is to read through your 15-minute lessons using the book only, and then go back and work with the audio and the book together, repeating the text in the gaps provided and then recording yourself. Or you can combine the book and the audio right from the beginning, pausing the app to read the instructions on the page as you need to. Try to say the words aloud, and practise enunciating properly. Detailed instructions on how to use the app are available from the menu bar in the app.

Remember that repetition is vital to language learning. The more often you listen to a conversation or repeat an oral exercise, the more the language will sink in.

Menu, Help/How to Use, Your Library

1 Getting started
The list of weeks will open when the audio has been downloaded. From here you can tap into each week's lessons.

When all the lessons in a week have been completed, the week button will be filled with color and show a check mark, so you can track your progress.

2 Lessons week by week
Each numbered exercise in a lesson is listed in the app as it appears in the book. Tap on an exercise to start.

A check mark indicates when an exercise has been completed.

3 Audio for exercises
Tap the play button to hear instructions, then the exercise. You can pause the audio at any point, and return to it.

You can tap any part of the exercise to play the audio from that point.

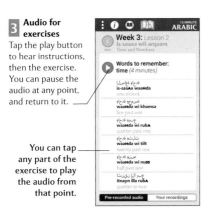

4 Record yourself
When you are in the Your recordings screen, you can record yourself reading the words or participating in the conversations with native speakers, then listen back (and rerecord if desired).

Add recording

Play recording

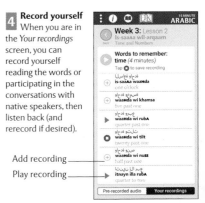

1 **Warm up** (1 minute)

The Warm Up panel appears at the beginning of each lesson. It will remind you of what you have already learned and prepare you for moving ahead with the new subject.

Ahlan
Hello

Arabs are generally very effusive on meeting. The wide variety of greetings are often accompanied by back-slapping, handshakes, hugging, and kissing. However, it is best to avoid physical contact with the opposite sex on first meeting to avoid causing any unintentional offense.

سلام.
salaam
Hi!

2 **Words to remember** (4 minutes)

Look at these greetings and say them aloud. Conceal the text on the left with the cover flap and try to remember the Arabic.

صباح الخير. *sabaaн il-khayr*	Good morning.
صباح النور. *sabaaн in-noor*	Good morning. (reply)
مساء الخير. *masaa il-khayr*	Good evening/ afternoon.
مساء النور. *masaa in-noor*	Good evening/ afternoon. (reply)
أنا اسمي... *ena ismee...*	My name is...
تشرّفنا. *tusharrafna*	Pleased to meet you.

3 **In conversation: formal** (4 minutes)

صباح الخير.
أنا اسمي مايك هولند.
sabaaн il-khayr. ena ismee mike holland

Good morning.
My name is Mike Holland.

صباح النور.
أنا اسمي أمينة هاشم.
sabaaн in-noor. ena ismee ameena haashim

Good morning.
My name is Amina Haashim.

تشرّفنا.
tusharrafna
Pleased to meet you.

4 Put into practice (2 minutes)

Join in this conversation. Read the Arabic beside the pictures and follow the instructions to make your reply. Then test yourself by concealing the answers on the right with the cover flap.

مساء النور   مساء الخير.
masaa in-noor   *masaa il-khayr*
Good evening.

Say: Good evening. (reply)

تشرّفنا   أنا اسمي أمير زكي.
tusharrafna   *ena ismee ameer zaki*
My name is Amir Zaki.

Say: Pleased to
meet you.

Conversational tip There are more than 20 countries, stretching from northwest Africa well into Asia, where Arabic is the official language. The formal language of the media and government is standard across these countries but informal spoken Arabic varies from region to region. It is spoken Arabic that you will need to use in everyday situations such as shopping and sightseeing. The Arabic taught in this book is essentially Egyptian spoken dialect. This is one of the most widely understood dialects throughout the Arab world; Egypt is the region's leading exporter of popular culture in the form of movies, television programs, and songs. However, some variations have been included to make the Arabic more widely applicable.

5 In conversation: informal (4 minutes)

سلام يا سامي!
salaam yaa saamee
Bye, Sami!

مع السلامة.
أشوفك بكرة.
maʌasalaama. ashoofik bukra
**Goodbye. See you
tomorrow.**

أيوه. مع السلامة.
aywah. maʌasalaama
Yes. Goodbye.

1 Warm up (1 minute)

Say "hello" and "goodbye" in Arabic. (pp.8-9)

Now say "My name is…" (pp.8-9)

Say "Pleased to meet you". (pp.8-9)

Il-Aela
Relatives

In Arabic, relatives are categorized according to whether they are related to the mother (maternal) or the father (paternal). The *maternal uncle* and *aunt* are **khaal** and **khAala**; the *paternal uncle* and *aunt* are **aamm** and **Aamma**. Cousins are referred to by the precise relationship: **ibn khaal** (*son of maternal uncle*), and so on.

2 Match and repeat (4 minutes)

Look at the people in this scene and match their numbers with the list at the side. Read the Arabic words aloud. Now, conceal the list with the cover flap and test yourself.

❶ ابن
ibn

❷ بنت
bint

❸ جد
gidd

❹ أب
ab

❺ أم
omm

❻ جدة
gidda

grandfather ❸

❹ father

❺ mother

❷ daughter

❶ son

grandmother ❻

Conversational tip Words referring to females often end in *-a* - for example, *gidda* (*grandmother*). In Arabic, things as well as people are masculine or feminine. Feminine things nearly always end with *-a* - for example, *kursee* (*chair*) is masculine but *ahwa* (*coffee*) is feminine.

3 Words to remember: relatives (4 minutes)

Familiarize yourself with these words and phrases. Read them aloud several times and try to memorize them. Conceal the Arabic with the cover flap and test yourself.

زوجة
zohga
wife

زوج
zohg
husband

brother	أخ *akh*	
sister	أخت *ukht*	
children	أولاد *awlaad*	
I have four children.	أنا عندي أربع أولاد. *ena Aandee arbaA awlaad*	
I have a boy and three girls.	أنا عندي ولد وثلاث بنات. *ena Aandee walad wi talat banaat*	

أنا متجوز/ة
ana mitgawwiz/-a
I'm married (m/f).

4 Words to remember: numbers (5 minutes)

Memorize these words and then test yourself using the cover flap.

Arabic plurals need to be learned individually. For example, the plural of **bint** (*girl*) is **banaat**; the plural of **walad** (*boy*) is **awlaad**, also used to mean *children*.

Numbers lose the final -**a** when put directly in front of another word: **talat banaat** (*three girls*).

A feature of Arabic is the "dual" ending. When talking about two of something, you don't usually use the number two, **itnayn**. Instead you put -**ayn** on the end of the word: **bintayn** (*two girls*).

one	واحد *waaHid*	
two	اثنين *itnayn*	
three	ثلاثة *talaata*	
four	أربعة *arbaAa*	
five	خمسة *khamsa*	
six	ستة *sitta*	
seven	سبعة *sabaAa*	
eight	ثمانية *tamanya*	
nine	تسعة *tisAa*	
ten	عشرة *Aashra*	

5 Say it (1 minute)

I have two boys.

I have three children.

I have a brother and two sisters.

1 Warm up (1 minute)

Say "See you tomorrow." (pp.8-9)

Say "I'm married" (pp.10-11) and "I have a brother." (pp.12-13)

Yikoon wi Aand
To be and to have

Arabic has a verb **yikoon** meaning *to be*, but it is usually omitted in the present. So, *he is from Egypt* is **huwa min muSr** (literally *he from Egypt*). For *I have, he has*, and so on, Arabic uses the word **Aand** (*at*) with one of the possessive endings (see page 12), as in **ena Aandee akh** (*I have a brother*).

2 Pronouns (5 minutes)

Familiarize yourself with how to say the Arabic pronouns. When you are confident, practice the sample sentences below.

ena	أنا	I [am]
enta/enti	أنتَ/أنتِ	you [are] (m/f)
huwa	هو	he [is]
heyya	هي	she [is]
iHna	احنا	we [are]
entum	أنتم	you [are] (pl)
humma	همّا	they [are]
أنتَ/أنتِ منين؟ *enta/enti minayn*	Where are you from? (to a male/female)	
أنتم منين؟ *entum minayn*	Where are you from? (to a couple or group)	

أنا بريطانية.
ena biriTaaneeya
I'm British.

Read it In Arabic script the writing runs right to left (look at the question marks in the panel above). There are 28 letters in the alphabet but no capital letters. All but six of the letters join up within a word. You don't normally "print" Arabic words using separated letters. In addition, most Arabic letters change their shape depending on their position in a word (the first letter, a middle letter, or the last letter). However, they usually retain some recognizable features wherever they appear. Look at how the Arabic words **ism** (*name*) and **gidd** (*grandfather*) are written (reading from right to left):

ا + س + م = اسم (*ism*)   ج + د = جد (*gidd*)

احنا من مصر.
iHna min muSr
We're from Egypt.

3 ʌand: to have (5 minutes)

Practice **ʌand** (*to have*) and the sample sentences, then test yourself. The pronoun is optional: (*ena*) **ʌandee** (*I have*); (*huwa*) **ʌanduh** (*he has*), etc.

I have	أنا عندي ena ʌandee
you have (m/f)	أنتَ عندَك/أنتِ عندِك enta ʌandak/enti ʌandik
he has	هو عنده huwa ʌanduh
she has	هي عندها heyya ʌandaha
we have	احنا عندنا iнna ʌandina
you have (pl)	أنتم عندكم entum ʌandukum
they have	همّا عندهم humma ʌanduhum

عندكم ورد أحمر؟
ʌandukum ward ʌнmar
Do you have red roses?

He has a meeting.	هو عنده اجتماع. huwa ʌanduh igtimaaʌ
Do you have a cell phone? (to a male)	أنتَ عندَك موبايل؟ enta ʌandak mubayil
How many brothers and sisters do you have? (to a female)	أنتِ عندِك كام أخ وأخت؟ enti ʌandik kaam akh w-ukht

4 Negatives (4 minutes)

A simple way to make sentences negative in Arabic is to use the word **mish** (*not*). The negative of (*ena*) **ʌandee** is (*ena*) **mʌandeesh** (*I don't have*).

I'm not British.	أنا مش بريطانية. ena mish biriтaaneeya
He's not vegetarian.	هو مش نباتي. huwa mish nabaatee
Are you (pl) not from Egypt?	أنتم مش من مصر؟ entum mish min musr
I don't have a sister.	أنا ماعنديش أخت. ena mʌandeesh ukht
I don't have children.	أنا ماعنديش أولاد. ena mʌandeesh awlaad

عجلة
ʌagala
bicycle

ماعنديش سيارة.
mʌandeesh sayyaara
I don't have a car.

il-agweba
Answers Cover with flap

RaagiA wi karrar
Review and repeat

il-agweba
Answers Cover with flap

1 How many?

❶ ثلاثة
talaata

❷ تسعة
tisAa

❸ أربعة
arbaAa

❹ اثنين
itnayn

❺ ثمانية
tamanya

❻ عشرة
Aashra

❼ خمسة
khamsa

❽ سبعة
sabaAa

❾ ستة
sitta

1 How many? (2 minutes)

Cover the answers with the flap. Then say these Arabic numbers out loud. Check you have remembered the Arabic correctly.

2 Hello

❶ صباح النور. أنا اسمي...
sabaaн in-noor.
ena ismee...

❷ تشرّفنا.
tusharrafna

❸ أنا عندي ولدين. وأنتم؟
ena Aandee waladayn.
w-entum

❹ مع السلامة.
أشوفِك بكرة.
maAasalaama.
ashoofik bukra

2 Hello (4 minutes)

You are talking to someone you have just met. Join in the conversation, replying in Arabic following the English prompts.

sabaaн il-khayr. ena ismee ameena haashim.
❶ Answer the greeting and give your name.
dah zohgee
❷ Say "Pleased to meet you."
enta Aandak awlaad?
❸ Say "Yes, I have two boys. And you?"
Aandina bintayn
❹ Say "Goodbye. See you tomorrow."

3 To have (5 minutes)

Fill in the blanks with the correct form of **Aand** (to have). Check you have remembered the Arabic correctly.

❶ *ena* _____ *akh*

❷ *iHna* _____ *sayyaara*

❸ *enta* _____ *awlaad?*

❹ *humma* _____ *ward aHmar?*

❺ *huwa* _____ *mubayil*

❻ *heyya* _____ *waladayn*

❼ *entum* _____ *ikhwaat?*

3 To have

❶ عندي
Aandee

❷ عندنا
Aandina

❸ عندَك
Aandak

❹ عندهم
Aanduhum

❺ عنده
Aanduh

❻ عندها
Aandaha

❼ عندكم
Aandukum

4 Family (4 minutes)

Say the Arabic for each of the numbered family members. Check you have remembered the Arabic correctly.

father ❶   mother ❷   ❸ daughter   ❺ grandmother   son ❻   grandfather ❹

4 Family

❶ أب
ab

❷ أم
omm

❸ بنت
bint

❹ جد
gidd

❺ جدة
gidda

❻ ابن
ibn

Warm up (1 minute)

Count to ten. (pp.10-11)

Remind yourself how to say "hello" and "goodbye." (pp.8-9)

Ask "Do you (plural) have any children?" (pp.14-15)

Fil kafiterya
In the coffee house

The traditional Arab café (**il-ahwa**), in the past mainly male-oriented, offers Arabic coffee or black tea, shisha (water or "hubble bubble") pipes, and perhaps a game of backgammon or dominoes. In recent times, modern coffee houses have sprung up, catering to customers of all ages and genders.

Words to remember (5 minutes)

Familiarize yourself with these phrases.

قهوة بدون حليب
ahwa bidoon нaleeb
black coffee

شاي بحليب *shay bi-нaleeb*	tea with milk
شاي بنعناع *shay bi-naʌnaaʌ*	mint tea
سندويتش *sandawitsh*	sandwich
توست ومربى *tost wi murabba*	toast and jam

Cultural tip Traditional Arabic coffee is served in a small cup, and is black and very strong. Brewed in a special jug, it comes in three basic styles: **saada** (*without sugar*); **mazboot** (*medium sweet*); and **ziyaada** (*very sweet*).

In conversation (4 minutes)

آخذ شاي بدون حليب.
aakhud ahwa bi-нaleeb min faɒlak

I'll have a coffee with milk, please.

حاجة ثانية؟
нaaga tanya

Anything else?

عندكم بسبوسة؟
ʌandukum basboosa

Do you have basboosa [semolina cake]?

تورتة
torta
cake

سكّر
sukkar
sugar

قهوة بحليب
ahwa bi-Haleeb
coffee with milk

4 Useful phrases (5 minutes)

Learn these phrases. Read the English under the pictures and say the phrase in Arabic as shown on the right. Then cover the Arabic with the flap and test yourself.

آخذ شاي بدون حليب.
aakhud shay bidoon Haleeb

I'll have a black tea.

حاجة ثانية؟
Haaga tanya

Anything else?

عندكم فول؟
Aandukum fool

Do you have mashed fava beans?

كام الحساب؟
kaam il-Hisaab

How much is the bill?

أيوه، عندنا.
aywah. Aandina
Yes, we do.

شكرا. كام الحساب من فضلك؟
shukran. kaam il-Hisaab min faDlak
Thank you. How much is the bill, please?

تسعة جنيه، من فضلك.
tisAa ginayh, min faDlak
Nine pounds, please.

Fil-matAam
In the restaurant

1 Warm up (1 minute)

Ask "How much is that?"
(pp.18-19)

Say "I don't have
a brother." (pp.14-15)

Ask "Do you have
fava beans?" (pp.18-19)

There are a huge variety of different types of eating
places in the Arab world—from traditional vendors
selling **fool** (*fava beans*) and **falaafil** (*chickpea balls*),
grilled **kofta** (*minced meat*), or **firaakh** (*chicken*) to
modern, Western-style five-star restaurants.

2 Words to remember (3 minutes)

Memorize these words. Conceal the Arabic
with the cover flap and test yourself.

7 cup

المنيو *il-menu*	menu
فواتح الشهية *fawaatiн ish- shaheyya*	appetizers
الطبق الرئيسي *iт-тaba' ir-rayeesee*	main course
الحلو *il-нilw*	dessert
الفطار *il-fiтaar*	breakfast
الغداء *il-ghada*	lunch
العشاء *il-ʌasha*	dinner

5 spoon

4 knife

6 fork

3 In conversation (4 minutes)

اهلا. مائدة لأربعة، من
فضلك.

*ahlan. maa'ida li-arbaʌa
min fadlak*

Hello. A table for
four, please.

عندكم حجز؟

ʌandukum нagz

Do you have
a reservation?

أيوه، بإسم مبروك.

aywah. bi-ism mabrook
Yes, in the name
of Mabrook.

4 Match and repeat (5 minutes)

Look at the numbered objects on this table and match them with the items in the vocabulary list at the side. Read the Arabic words aloud. Now, conceal the list with the cover flap and test yourself.

❶ كوب
koob

❷ فوطة
foo-тa

❸ طبق
тaba'

❹ سكين
sikkeen

❺ ملعقة
malʌa'a

❻ شوكة
shohka

❼ فنجان
fingaan

❶ glass

❷ napkin

❸ plate

5 Useful phrases (2 minutes)

Learn these phrases and then test yourself using the cover flap to conceal the Arabic.

What desserts do you have?	عندكم إيه حلو؟ *ʌandukum eh нilw*
The check, please.	الحساب من فضلك. *il-нisaab, min faдlak*

تدخين أو دون تدخين؟
tadkheen aw doon tadkheen

Smoking or non-smoking?

دون تدخين.
doon tadkheen

Non-smoking.

اتفضلوا هنا.
ittafaддaloo hina

Please [sit] over here.

1 Warm up (1 minute)

What are "breakfast," "lunch," and "dinner" in Arabic? (pp.20-1)

Say "I," "you" (masculine), "you" (feminine), "he," "she," "we," "you" (plural), "they." (pp.14-15)

Aawiz
To want

Aawiz literally means *wanting* and can be used to make requests: ***ena Aawiz il-menu min faɒlak*** (*I want the menu, please*); if it is clear who you are referring to, you can drop the pronoun: ***Aawiz ahwa?*** (*Do you want coffee?*). Use **Aawza** if you are referring to a female, and **Aawzeen** for groups.

2 Aawiz: to want (6 minutes)

Say the different forms of **Aawiz** aloud. When you are confident, use the cover flap to test yourself.

أنا عاوز	I want (m)
ena Aawiz	
أنا عاوزة	I want (f)
ena Aawza	
أنت عاوز	you want (m)
enta Aawiz	
أنت عاوزة	you want (f)
enti Aawza	
هو عاوز	he wants
huwa Aawiz	
هي عاوزة	she wants
heyya Aawza	
احنا عاوزين	we want
iнna Aawzeen	
أنتم عاوزين	you want (pl)
entum Aawzeen	
همّا عاوزين	they want
humma Aawzeen	

همّا عاوزين شوكولاتة؟
humma Aawzeen shokolaata
Do they want chocolates?

Conversational tip

The Arabic phrase **min faɒlak** (*please*) literally means *from your grace*; **min** means *from*, and **faɒl** means *grace*. The ending **-ak** means *your* when talking to a male (see pp.12-13). When talking to a female, use the ending **-ik** (**min faɒlik**) and, when talking to a group, use **-ukum** (**min faɒlukum**).

3 Polite requests (4 minutes)

You can use the word **mumkin...?** (*possible...?*) to mean *can I/we have...?*,
adding **min faɒlak** (*please*) to make your request sound more polite
(see Conversational tip). Practice the following sample phrases.

Can I have a juice, please? (asking a male)	ممكن عصير، من فضلك؟ **mumkin Aaseer, min faɒlak**
Can I have a table for tonight, please? (asking a female)	ممكن مائدة الليلة، من فضلك؟ **mumkin maa'ida il-layla, min faɒlik**
Can we have the menu, please? (asking a group)	ممكن المنيو، من فضلكم؟ **mumkin il-menu, min faɒlukum**

4 Put into practice (4 minutes)

Join in this conversation. Read the Arabic beside the pictures and follow the
instructions to make your reply. Then test yourself by concealing the answers
using the cover flap.

مساء الخير. عندكم حجز؟
masaa il-khayr.
Aandak Hagz

Good evening. Do you have a reservation?

Say: No, but can I have a table for three, please?

لا، بس ممكن مائدة لثلاثة، من فضلك؟
laa, bass mumkin maa'ida li-talaata, min faɒlak

حاضر. عاوز أي واحدة؟
Haaɒir. Aawiz ayya waHda

Certainly. Which one do you want?

Say: Near the window, please.

جنب الشباك، من فضلك.
ganb ish-shibaak, min faɒlak

Il-aTbaa'
Dishes

Dishes vary from region to region in the Arabic-speaking world, but much of the cooking is grilled or stewed. Not many restaurants offer a vegetarian menu, but there are many traditional Arabic dishes that do not contain meat or can be prepared without it. Ask your waiter for advice.

Cultural tip
In the Middle East you can make a whole meal out of bread and starters such as *falafel* (chick pea balls), *fool* (mashed fava beans), *нumus* (mashed chick peas), and many more.

Match and repeat (6 minutes)

Match the numbered items to the Arabic words in the panel and test yourself using the cover flap.

❶ خضار
khuɒaar

❷ فواكه
fawaakih

❸ جبنة
gibna

❹ مكسرات
mukassaraat

❺ شوربة
shorba

❻ فراخ
firaakh

❼ سمك
samak

❽ مكرونة
makarona

❾ فواكه البحر
fawaakih il-baнr

❿ لحمة
laнma

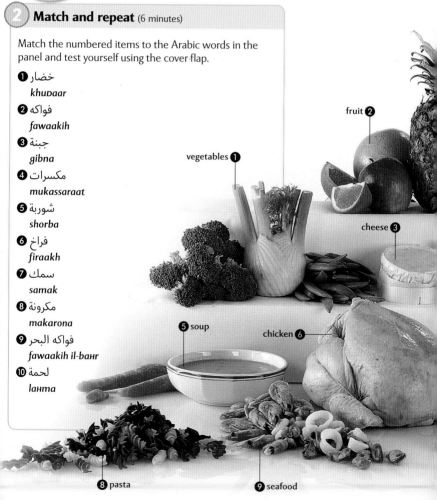

fruit **❷**

vegetables **❶**

cheese **❸**

❺ soup

chicken **❻**

❽ pasta

❾ seafood

3 **Words to remember: cooking methods** (3 minutes)

Memorize these words. Conceal the Arabic with the cover flap and test yourself.

fried	مقلي
	ma'lee
grilled	مشوي
	mashwee
roasted	في الفرن
	fil-furn
boiled	مسلوق
	masloo'
in tomato sauce	بالصلصة
	bis-salsa

ممكن لحمة مشوية؟

mumkin laнma mashweyya

Can I have grilled meat?

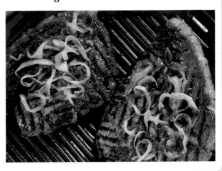

5 **Say it** (2 minutes)

Can I have fried fish?

He wants soup.

I want pasta.

Do you want chicken?

nuts **4**

fish **7**

10 meat

4 **Words to remember: drinks** (3 minutes)

Familiarize yourself with these words and use the cover flap to test yourself.

(mineral) water	مياه (معدنية)
	mayya (maʌdaneyya)
tamarind drink	تمر هندي
	tamru hindi
wine	نبيذ
	nibeet
beer	بيرة
	beera
juice	عصير
	ʌaseer

Read it In Arabic script, as in phone texting, many vowels are not written. For example, the Arabic word **mumkin** (*possible*) is written as "mmkn" and **samak** (*fish*) as "smk." It is possible to show the vowels as marks above and below the main script, but in most cases, written Arabic omits these. Look at the elements that make up these two words and the alternative written forms with and without vowels. (Read the breakdowns from right to left.)

م + م + ك + ن = ممكن or مُمْكِن (mumkin)

س + م + ك = سمك or سَمَك (samak)

RaagiA wi karrar
Review and repeat

1 What food?

❶ مكسرات
mukassaraat

❷ فواكه البحر
fawaakih il-baнr

❸ لحمة
laнma

❹ سكر
sukkar

❺ كوب
koob

1 What food? (4 minutes)

Name the numbered items.

- ❶ nuts
- ❷ seafood
- ❸ meat
- ❹ sugar
- ❺ glass

2 This is my...

❶ دي زوجتي.
dee zohgtee

❷ ده زوجها؟
dah zohg-ha

❸ دي بنتنا.
dee bintina

❹ ده ابنَك؟
dah ibnak

2 This is my... (4 minutes)

Say these phrases in Arabic.

❶ This is my wife.

❷ Is that her husband?

❸ That's our daughter.

❹ Is this your son?
(talking to a male)

3 Can I have...

❶ ممكن قهوة بدون حليب؟
mumkin ahwa bidoon наleeb

❷ ممكن تورتة؟
mumkin torta

❸ ممكن سكر؟
mumkin sukkar

❹ ممكن قهوة بالحليب؟
mumkin ahwa bil-наleeb

3 Can I have... (3 minutes)

Say "Can I have?" the following:

- ❶ black coffee
- ❷ cake
- ❸ sugar
- ❹ white coffee

il-agweba
Answers Cover with flap

pasta ⑥

knife ⑦

⑧ cheese

juice ⑩

⑨ napkin

What food?

❻ مكرونة
makarona

❼ سكين
sikkeen

❽ جبنة
gibna

❾ فوطة
foo-тa

❿ عصير
лaseer

Restaurant (4 minutes)

You arrive at a restaurant. Join in the conversation, replying in Arabic following the English prompts.

masaa il-khayr
❶ Ask for a table for six.

tadkheen aw doon tadkheen?
❷ Say: non-smoking.

ittafaлoaloo hina
❸ Ask for the menu.

лawzeen mayya maлdaneyya?
❹ Say: No. Tamarind drink, please.

нaaоir
❺ Say: I don't have a glass.

Restaurant

❶ مائدة لستة، من فضلك.
maa'ida li-sitta, min faлlak

❷ دون تدخين.
doon tadkheen

❸ ممكن المنيو؟
mumkin il-menu

❹ لا، تمر هندي، من فضلك.
laa. tamru hindi, min faлlak

❺ ماعنديش كوب.
ma лandeesh koob

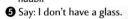

Il-ayyaam wish-shuhoor
Days and months

1 Warm up (1 minute)

Say "He is vegetarian" and "I have a bicycle." (pp.14–15)

Say "She is not from Egypt" and "I don't have a car." (pp.14–15)

What is the Arabic for "children"? (pp.10–11)

Sometimes the word **yohm** (day) is used in front of the days of the week—for example, **yohm il-itnayn** (Monday). Friday is the main day off in the Middle East, with offices and schools also sometimes closed on Saturday.

2 Words to remember: days of the week (5 minutes)

Familiarize yourself with these words and test yourself using the flap.

الأثنين	Monday
il-itnayn	
الثلاثاء	Tuesday
it-talaat	
الأربعاء	Wednesday
il-arbaʌa	
الخميس	Thursday
il-khamees	
الجمعة	Friday
il-gumʌa	
السبت	Saturday
is-sabt	
الأحد	Sunday
il-Had	
النهاردة	today
innahaarda	

الاجتماع بكرة.
il-igtimaaʌ bukra
The meeting is tomorrow.

عندي حجز للنهاردة.
ʌandee Hagz l-innahaarda
I have a reservation for today.

3 Useful phrases: days (2 minutes)

Learn these phrases and then test yourself using the cover flap.

الاجتماع مش يوم الثلاثاء.
il-igtimaaʌ mish yohm it-talaat

The meeting isn't on Tuesday.

باشتغل يوم الجمعة.
bashtaghil yohm il-gumʌa

I work on Fridays.

4 Words to remember: months (5 minutes)

Familiarize yourself with these words and test yourself using the flap.

عيد زواجنا في يوليو.
ʌeed zawaagna fi yoolyo
Our wedding anniversary is in July.

رمضان شهر الصوم.
ramaʌaan shahr is-sohm
Ramadan is the month of fasting.

January	يناير	*yanaayir*
February	فبراير	*febraayir*
March	مارس	*maaris*
April	أبريل	*abreel*
May	مايو	*maayo*
June	يونيو	*yoonyo*
July	يوليو	*yoolyo*
August	أغسطس	*aghusʈus*
September	سبتمبر	*sebtembir*
October	أكتوبر	*oktobir*
November	نوفمبر	*nofembir*
December	ديسمبر	*disembir*

5 Useful phrases: months (2 minutes)

Learn these phrases and then test yourself using the cover flap.

My children have a holiday in August.

أولادي عندهم اجازة في أغسطس.
awlaadee ʌanduhum agaaza fi aghusʈus

My birthday is in June.

عيد ميلادي في يونيو.
ʌeed milaadee fi yoonyo

1 Warm up (1 minute)

Count in Arabic from 1 to 10. (pp.10-11)

Say "I have a reservation." (pp.20-1)

Say "The meeting is on Wednesday." (pp.28-9)

Is-saaAa wil-arqaam
Time and numbers

The Arabic word **saaAa** means *hour* or *watch*, and is used for telling the time: **is-saaAa talaata** *three o'clock* "the hour three;" **is-saaAa kaam?** *what's the time?* "the hour how many?". In Arabic the hour comes first: **itnayn illa khamsa** ("two except five"–*five to two*). Twenty minutes is referred to as **tilt** (*a third*).

2 Words to remember: time (4 minutes)

Memorize how to tell the time in Arabic.

الساعة واحدة *is-saaAa waaнda*	one o'clock	
واحدة وخمسة *waaнda wi khamsa*	five past one	
واحدة وربع *waaнda wi rubA*	quarter past one	
واحدة وثلث *waaнda wi tilt*	twenty past one ["one and a third"]	
واحدة ونص *waaнda wi nuss*	half past one	
اثنين إلا ربع *itnayn illa rubA*	quarter to two	
اثنين إلا عشرة *itnayn illa Aashra*	ten to two	

3 Useful phrases (2 minutes)

Learn these phrases and then test yourself using the cover flap.

الساعة كام؟ *is-saaAa kaam*	What time is it?
عاوزين الفطار الساعة كام؟ *Aawzeen il-fiтaar is-saaAa kaam*	What time do you want breakfast?
الاجتماع الساعة اثنا عشر. *il-igtimaaA is-saaAa itnAashar*	The meeting is at 12 o'clock.

4 Words to remember: higher numbers (6 minutes)

For the numbers from 20 to 99 in Arabic, say the units first followed by the tens, linking the numbers with **wi** (*and*)—for example, **waahid wi Aishreen** (21, "one and twenty"); **sitta wi talaateen** (36, "six and thirty"); **tamanya wi sabaAeen** (78, "eight and seventy").

A *thousand* is **elf**. The dual ending **-ayn** (see pp.10-11) is used for *200* (**miyatayn**) and *2,000* (**elfayn**).

eleven	احدى عشر	**HidAashar**
twelve	اثنا عشر	**itnAashar**
thirteen	ثلاثة عشر	**talatAashar**
fourteen	أربعة عشر	**arbaatAashar**
fifteen	خمسة عشر	**khamastAashar**
sixteen	ستة عشر	**sittAashar**
seventeen	سبعة عشر	**sabaAATAashar**
eighteen	ثمانية عشر	**tamantAashar**
nineteen	تسعة عشر	**tisATAashar**
twenty	عشرين	**Aishreen**
thirty	ثلاثين	**talaateen**
forty	أربعين	**arbaAeen**
fifty	خمسين	**khamseen**
sixty	ستين	**sitteen**
seventy	سبعين	**sabaAeen**
eighty	ثمانين	**tamaneen**
ninety	تسعين	**tisAeen**
hundred	مائة	**mia**

أنا عاوز الأوتوبيس نمرة ثلاثة وخمسين.

ena Aawiz il-otobees nimra talaata wi khamseen

I want the number 53 bus.

5 Say it (2 minutes)

25

68

84

91

five to ten.

twenty past eleven.

What time is lunch?

Il-mawaΛeed
Appointments

1 Warm up (1 minute)

Say the days of the week.
(pp.28-9)

Say "three o'clock."
(pp.30-1)

What's the Arabic for
"today" and "tomorrow"?
(pp.28-9)

For a foreigner, conducting business in the Arab world can require a considerable amount of tact and patience. The traditional notion of hospitality also extends to business situations. You may well be offered drinks and snacks at meetings and it is polite to accept them.

سلام باليد
salaam bil-yad
handshake

مرحب
marΗab
Welcome.

2 Useful phrases (5 minutes)

Learn these phrases and then test yourself using the cover flap.

نتقابل بكرة؟ *nit'aabil bukra*	Shall we meet tomorrow?
مع مين؟ *maΛa meen*	With whom?
أنت فاضي امتى؟ *enta faaDi imta*	When are you free?
آسف، أنا مشغول. *aasif, ena mashghool*	Sorry, I am busy.
الخميس كويس؟ *il-khamees kwayyis*	Is Thursday OK?
أيوه ده يناسبني. *aywa, dah yinaasibnee*	That suits me.

3 In conversation (4 minutes)

مساء الخير.
أنا عندي ميعاد.
masaa il-khayr.
ena Λandee miΛaad

Good afternoon. I have an appointment.

ميعادك مع مين؟
miΛaadak maΛa meen

Who is your appointment with?

مع الأستاذ حسن.
maΛa l-ustaaz Ηasan

With Mr. Hassan.

4 Put into practice (5 minutes)

Join in this conversation. Read the Arabic beside the pictures on the left and then follow the instructions to make your reply. Then test yourself by concealing the answers on the right with the cover flap.

نتقابل الخميس؟
nit'aabil il-khamees
Shall we meet Thursday?

Say: Sorry, I'm busy.

آسف، أنا مشغول. /
آسفة، أنا مشغولة.
aasif, ena mashghool/
aasfa, ena mashghoola
(m/f)

يناسبك امتى؟
yinaasabak imta
When suits you?

Say: Tuesday afternoon.

الثلاثاء بعد الظهر.
it-talaat baʌd iḍ-ḍuhr

Conversational tip

If you are talking as a female or to a female, you need to add the ending **-a** to descriptive words such as **aasif** (sorry), **faaḍi** (free), **mashghool** (busy), and **mitakh-khar** (late). A woman would say: **aasfa, ena mashgoola** (Sorry, I am busy) or **ena mitakh-khara** (I am late). You would ask a woman **enti faaḍya?** (Are you free?).

الساعة كام ميعادك؟
is-saaʌa kaam miʌaadak

What time is your appointment?

الساعة ثلاثة، بس أنا متأخر.
is-saaʌa talaata, bass ena mitakh-khar

Three o'clock, but I'm late.

معلش. اتفضل استريح.
maʌalesh. itfaḍḍal estarayyaн

Never mind. Please take a seat.

1 **Warm up** (1 minute)

Say "I'm sorry." (pp.32-3)

What is the Arabic for "I have an appointment."? (pp.32-3)

How do you say "when?" in Arabic? (pp.32-3)

Aalat-tilifohn
On the telephone

Public telephones are becoming less common in many countries. If you think you will need to make a lot of phone calls, it is often a good idea to buy a local SIM card for your cell phone. Emergency and directory numbers vary from country to country.

2 **Match and repeat** (4 minutes)

Match the numbered items to the Arabic in the panel on the left, then test yourself.

❶ شاحن
shaaHin

❷ أنسر
ansar

❸ تليفون
tilifohn

❹ موبايل
mubayil

❺ سماعات
sammaaAAat

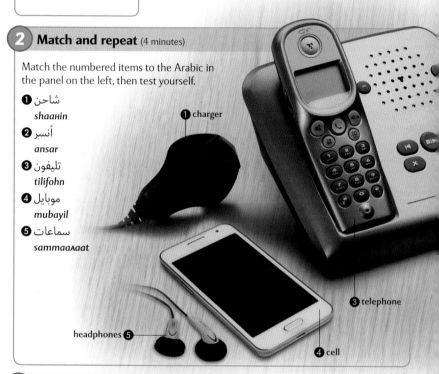

❶ charger

❸ telephone

headphones ❺

❹ cell

3 **In conversation** (4 minutes)

آلو. معاك عزة بركات.
aaloh. maAAak Azza barakaat

Hello. Azza Barakat speaking.

ممكن أكلم الأستاذ بدران من فضلك؟
mumkin akallim il-ustaaz badraan, min faɒlik

Can I speak to Mr. Badraan, please?

مين معايا؟
meen maAAaya

Who's calling?

4 Useful phrases (4 minutes)

Practice these phrases and then test yourself using the cover flap.

أنا آسف. النمرة غلط.
ena aasif, in-nimra ghalaт

I'm sorry, wrong number.

ممكن أشتري سمكارت محلي؟
mumkin ashtari sim-kart манаllee
Can I buy a local SIM card?

ممكن أسيب رسالة؟
mumkin aseeb risaala

Can I leave a message?

● ② answering machine

Read it

Most Arabic letters are joined to those before and after it in a word. When a letter comes last in a word, it usually has a "tail" or some kind of flourish. For example, the letters **g** (*s*) and **k** (*sh*) have a left-hand tail, but lose this when not the final letter, leaving just the small "w" shape (with three dots above for **sh**):

maaris (March) مارس = س + ر + ا + م

aasif (sorry) آسف = ف + س + آ

shaaнin (charger) شاحن = ن + ح + ا + ش

See how many instances of the letters **g** (*s*) and **k** (*sh*) you can spot in this lesson.

5 Say it (2 minutes)

Can I speak to Mr Hassan?

Can I buy a charger?

هاري نولز من مطابع كابيتال.
haaree noolz min маτaabia kabitaal

Harry Knowles from Capital Printers.

أنا آسفة. الخط مشغول.
ena aasfa. il-khaтт mashghool

I'm sorry. The line is busy.

حاتصل بعدين.
натassil baдdayn
I'll call back later.

RaagiA wi karrar
Review and repeat

1 Sums

❶ ستة عشر
sittAashar

❷ سبعة وثلاثين
sabaAa wi-talateen

❸ ثلاثة وخمسين
talaata
wi-khamseen

❹ أربعة وسبعين
arbaAa
wi-sabaAeen

1 Sums (4 minutes)

Say the answers to
these sums out loud in
Arabic. Then check you
have remembered
correctly.

❶ 10 + 6 = ?
❷ 14 + 25 = ?
❸ 66 − 13 = ?
❹ 40 + 34 = ?

3 Telephones (3 minutes)

What are the numbered
items in Arabic?

cell ❶

headphones ❺

2 I want...

❶ عاوز
Aawiz

❷ عاوزة
Aawza

❸ عاوزين
Aawzeen

❹ عاوزين
Aawzeen

❺ عاوز
Aawiz

❻ عاوزة
Aawza

2 I want... (3 minutes)

Fill the gaps with
the correct form
of Aawiz (want).

❶ huwa _____ ahwa
❷ heyya _____ mayya
❸ iHna _____ Aaseer
❹ hum _____ shokolaata?
❺ enta _____ shay?
❻ enti _____ eh?

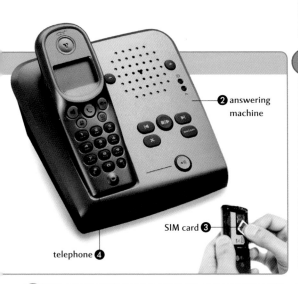

answering machine ②

SIM card ③

telephone ④

il-agweba
Answers Cover with flap

3 Telephones

① موبايل
mubayil

② أنسر
ansar

③ سمكارت
sim-kart

④ تليفون
tilifohn

⑤ سماعات
sammaaʌaat

---

4 When? (2 minutes)

What do these sentences mean?

① *ena ʌandee igtimaaʌ yohm il-itnayn*

② *ʌeed milaadee fi septembir*

③ *innahaarda il-gumʌa*

④ *bashtaghil yohm il-ħad*

4 When?

① I have a meeting on Monday.

② My birthday is in September.

③ Today is Friday.

④ I work on Sundays.

---

5 Time (3 minutes)

Say these times in Arabic.

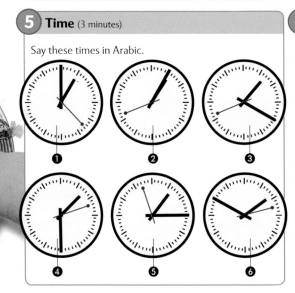

5 Time

① الساعة واحدة
is-saaʌa waaħda

② واحدة وخمسة
waaħda wi khamsa

③ واحدة وثلث
waaħda wi tilt

④ واحدة ونص
waaħda wi nuss

⑤ واحدة وربع
waaħda wi rubʌ

⑥ اثنين إلا عشرة
itnayn illa ʌshra

Fi shibbaak it-tazaakir
At the ticket office

The plural of *tazkara* (ticket) is *tazaakir*: *talat tazaakir l-aswaan* (*three tickets to Aswan*). *Two tickets* is *tazkartayn*, an example of the final *a* of *tazkara* changing to *t* when the dual ending *-ayn* is added (see pp.11–12).

---

1 **Warm up** (1 minute)

Count to 100 in tens. (pp.10–11, pp.30–1)

Ask "What time is it?" (pp.30–1)

Say "Half past one." (pp.30–1)

---

2 **Words to remember** (3 minutes)

Learn these words and then test yourself.

محطة القطار *мана́ттіт il-'атr*	train station
محطة الأوتوبيس *мана́ттіt il-ohtobees*	bus station
تذكرة *tazkara*	ticket
ذهاب *dhahaab*	single
ذهاب وعودة *dhahaab w-ʌawda*	round-trip
درجة أولى *daraga oola*	first class
درجة ثانية *daraga tanya*	second class

قطار   ركاب   رصيف
'атr   *rukkaab*   *raseef*
train   passengers   platform

المحطة زحمة.
il-мана́тта зана́та
The station is crowded.

---

3 **In conversation** (4 minutes)

تذكرتين للأقصر،
من فضلك.
*tazkartayn li-lu'sur,
min faɒlik*

Two tickets to
Luxor, please.

ذهاب وعودة؟
dhahaab w-ʌawda

Round-trip?

أيوه. لازم نحجز كراسي؟
aywah. laazim niнgiz karaasi

Yes. Do we have to
reserve seats?

4 **Useful phrases** (5 minutes)

Learn these phrases and then test yourself using the cover flap.

القطار متأخر.
il-'aTr mitakh-khar
The train is late.

لوحة
lawHa
sign

إلى أرصفة
٨ - ٦ - ٥
To PLATFORMS NO
5 - 6 - 8

How much is a ticket to Aswan?	بكام التذكرة لأسوان؟ *bikaam it-tazkara l-aswaan*
Two tickets to Cairo, please.	تذكرتين للقاهرة، من فضلك. *tazkartayn lil-qaahira, min fadlak*
Do I have to change trains?	لازم أغير القطار؟ *laazim aghayyir il-'aTr*
Can I pay by card?	ممكن أدفع بالكارت؟ *mumkin adfaA bil-kart*
Do we have to reserve seats?	لازم نحجز كراسي؟ *laazim niHgiz karaasi*
What time is the train for Alexandria?	قطار اسكندرية الساعة كام؟ *'aTr iskindereyya is-saAaa kaam*

5 **Say it** (2 minutes)

What time is the train to Aswan?

How much is a ticket to Luxor?

Cultural tip

Traveling by train in the Arab world may be less glamorous than in the past but it can still be an economic alternative to air travel. Many tourists enjoy taking a comfortable *sleeper car* (**arabit nohm**) from Cairo to Luxor or Aswan.

لا مش مهم.
ستين جنيه من فضلك.
laa mish muhimm.
sitteen gunayh min faDlik

No, that's not necessary.
Sixty pounds, please.

ممكن أدفع بالكارت؟
mumkin adfaA bil-kart
Can I pay by card?

إيوه ممكن. رصيف
نمرة خمسة.
aywah mumkin. raseef
nimra khamsa

Yes, you can. Platform
number five.

What is "train" in Arabic? (pp.38-9)

What does "**bikaam it-tazkara l-aswaan?**" mean? (pp.38-9)

Ask a male and a female "When are you free?" (pp.32-3)

Raayiн wi aakhid
Going and taking

RaayiH and *aakhud* mean *going* and *taking* and are placed directly after the subject, without the need for *am*, *is*, or *are*. As with *Aawiz* (*want*), you will need to add *-a* for a female and *-een* for a group: *huwa raayiн* (*he is going*); *ommee раауна* (*my mother is going*); *humma aakhdeen* (*they are taking*).

2 raayiн: going (6 minutes)

The pronoun isn't needed if the subject is clear. However, you should use the correct form of **raayiн** for a male, a female, or a group: *raayiн/раауна/raayнeen fayn? where are you going?* (masculine/feminine/plural)

أنا رايح/رايحة	ena raayiн/раауна	I am going (m/f)
أنت رايح	enta raayiн	you are going (m)
أنت رايحة	enti раауна	you are going (f)
هو رايح	huwa raayiн	he is going
هي رايحة	heyya раауна	she is going
احنا رايحين	iнna raayнeen	we are going
انتم رايحين	entum raayнeen	you are going (pl)
همّا رايحين	humma raayнeen	they are going

أنا رايح الجيزة.
ena raayiн ig-geeza
I'm going to Giza.

Conversational tip

You may have noticed that when you add *-a* for a female or *-een* for a group to *raayiн* (*going*), *aakhid* (*taking*), or *Aawiz* (*want*), the *i* sound disappears. Although strictly the combination produces, for example, *raayiнa* and *Aawizeen*, in everyday speech the sounds are compressed to become "*раауна*", "*Aawzeen*", and so on: *humma Aawzeen tazkartayn* (*they want two tickets*); *heyya раауна ig-geeza* (*she's going to Giza*).

③ aakhid: taking (6 minutes)

Say these short phrases aloud. Use the cover flap to test yourself. When you are confident, practice the longer sentences below.

احنا آخذين المترو النهاردة.
iнna aakhdeen il-metro innahaarda

We're taking the metro today.

أنا آخذ/آخذة *ena aakhid/aakhda*	I am taking (m/f)
أنت آخذ/أنتِ آخذة *enta aakhid/enti aakhda*	you are taking (m/f)
هو آخذ *huwa aakhid*	he is taking
هي آخذة *heyya aakhda*	she is taking
انتم/همّا/احنا آخذين *iнna/entum/ humma aakhdeen*	we/you (pl)/they are taking

هو مش آخذ تاكسي. *huwa mish aakhid taaksi*	He's not taking a taxi.
انتم آخذين الأوتوبيس؟ *entum aakhdeen il-otohbees*	Are you (pl) taking the bus?

④ Put into practice (2 minutes)

Cover the text on the right and complete the dialog in Arabic.

رايح فين؟
raayiн fayn
Where are you going?

أنا رايح الأقصر.
ena raayiн lu'sur
Say: I'm going to Luxor.

أنت آخذ تاكسي؟
enta aakhid taaksi
Are you taking a taxi?

لا، أنا آخذ القطار.
laa. ena aakhid il-'aтr
Say: No, I'm taking the train.

Taaksi, otohbees, wi metro
Taxi, bus, and metro

1 Warm up (1 minute)

Say "I'm not taking a taxi." (pp.40-1)

Ask a group of people "Where are you going?" (pp.40-1)

Say "80" and "40". (pp.30-1)

Egyptians generally use the word **otohbees** for *bus*, but in other regions you might hear **baas** or the more official **ʜaafila**. You may also be able to catch a microbus or a shared taxi, depending on where you want to go.

2 Words to remember (4 minutes)

Familiarize yourself with these words and test yourself using the cover flap.

أوتوبيس *otohbees*	bus/coach
شباك تذاكر *shibbaak tazaakir*	ticket office
محطة مترو *maʜattit metro*	metro station
موقف أوتوبيس *mawqaf otohbees*	bus stop
أجرة تاكسي *ogrit taaksi*	taxi fare
موقف تاكسي *mawqaf taaksi*	taxi stand

نمرة ١٧ يقف هنا؟
nimra sabaʌtaʌshar bi-yu'uf hina

Does the number 17 stop here?

3 In conversation: taxi (2 minutes)

خان الخليلي من فضلك.
Khan il-khalilee min faɒlak

Khan il-khalili, please.

ماشي. اتفضل.
maashi. ittafaɒɒal

OK. Please get in.

ممكن أنزل هنا من فضلك؟
mumkin anzil hina min faɒlak

Can I get out here, please?

4 Useful phrases (4 minutes)

Practice these phrases and then test yourself using the cover flap.

I want a taxi to Karnak.
عاوز تاكسي للكرنك.
ʌawiz taaksi lil-karnak

When is the next bus?
امتى الأوتوبيس الجاي؟
imta il-otohbees ig-gaay

How do I get to the museum?
ازاي أوصل المتحف؟
izzay awsal il-metнaf

How far is it?
المسافة قد إيه؟
il-misaafa adda eh

Please wait for me.
استناني من فضلك.
istanaanee min faдlak

Cultural tip There is a metro system in Cairo with lines identified by color. The Red and Blue Lines run north to south and the Green Line runs east to west. Expansion is planned but the network is currently limited. However, if your destination is on a metro line, you can avoid the traffic jams above ground.

6 Say it (2 minutes)

Does the number 6 stop here?

Are you going to Khan il-khalili?

How do I get to the train station?

5 In conversation: bus (2 minutes)

رايح عند المتحف؟
raayiн ʌand il-metнaf

Are you going to the museum?

أيوه. جنيه من فضلك.
awyah. ginayh min faдlik

Yes. A pound please.

قوللي لما نوصل.
ullee lama nohsil

Tell me when we arrive.

1 **Warm up** (1 minute)

Say "I have..."
(pp.14-15)

Say "my father," "my
sister," and "my son."
(pp.10-11, pp.12-13)

Say "I'm going to Luxor."
(pp.40-1)

AalaT-Tareeq
On the road

Self-drive car rental is not popular in the Middle East,
although it is possible for the adventurous traveler to
do this. It is more relaxing to hire a car with a driver.
If you decide to drive yourself, stick to the daytime,
be clear about the route, and learn to recognize
your destination in Arabic script.

2 **Match and repeat** (4 minutes)

Match the numbered items
to the list on the left, then
test yourself.

1 شنطة
shanta

2 بربريز
barabreez

3 كبوت
kabboot

4 عجلة
Aagala

5 كاوتش
kawitsh

6 باب
baab

7 فانوس
fanoos

8 اكسدام
iksiDaam

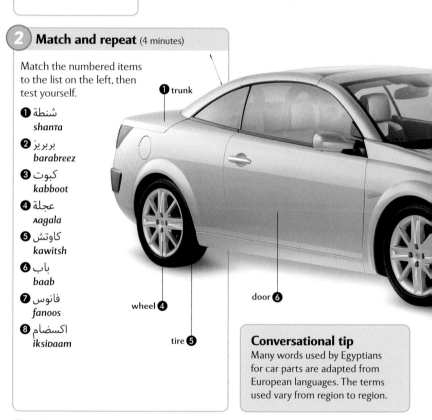

1 trunk

door **6**

wheel **4**

tire **5**

Conversational tip

Many words used by Egyptians
for car parts are adapted from
European languages. The terms
used vary from region to region.

3 **Road features** (2 minutes)

ميدان
midaan
square/traffic circle

إشارة
ishaara
traffic lights

شرطي المرور
shurTee il-muroor
traffic policeman

4 Useful phrases (4 minutes)

Learn these phrases and then test yourself using the cover flap.

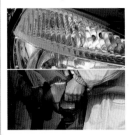

The turn signal isn't working.	الإشارة مش شغالة. *il-ishaara mish shagh-ghaala*
Fill it up, please.	املاها من فضلك. *imlaaha min faдlak*

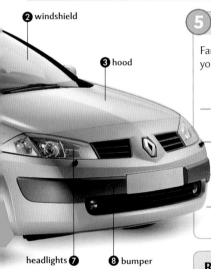

❷ windshield
❸ hood
headlights ❼   ❽ bumper

5 Words to remember (3 minutes)

Familiarize yourself with these words then test yourself using the flap.

gas	بنزين *benzeen*
diesel	ديزل *deezil*
oil	زيت *zayt*
engine	موتور *motoor*
license	رخصة *rukhsa*

Read it Six of the 28 letters of the Arabic alphabet are never joined to the next (left-hand) letter in a word: د (*d*); ذ (*z/d*); ر (*r*); ز (*z*); و (*w/oo*); ا (*a/aa*). This makes them easier to recognize as they don't significantly change their shapes. Look, for example, at the word ميدان (*midaan*), which contains both د and ا.

6 Say it (1 minute)

The headlights aren't working.

I don't have gaas.

كوبري علوي
kubree Aulwee

overpass

التول
it-tol

toll gate

زحمة مرور
zaнmit muroor

traffic jam

il-agweba
Answers Cover with flap

RaagiA wi karrar
Review and repeat

1 Transport

❶ أوتوبيس
otohbees

❷ تاكسي
taaksi

❸ عجلة
Aagala

❹ مترو
metro

❺ سيارة
sayyaara

1 Transport (3 minutes)

Name these forms of transport in Arabic.

bus ❶

car ❺

2 Going/taking

❶ رايحة
raayнa

❷ رايحين
raayнeen

❸ رايح
raayiн

❹ آخذين
aakhdeen

❺ آخذة
aakhda

❻ آخذ
aakhid

2 Going/taking (4 minutes)

Use the correct form of the word in brackets.

❶ enti ____ fayn? (raayiн)

❷ humma ____ ig-geeza (raayiн)

❸ huwa ____ il-metнaf (raayiн)

❹ entum ____ il-metro? (aakhid)

❺ heyya mish ____ taaksi (aakhid)

❻ enta ____ il-otohbees? (aakhid)

② taxi

④ metro

bicycle **③**

③ You? (4 minutes)

Use the correct phrase for *you* (**enta**, **enti**, or **entum**) in each question.

① Ask a male "Do you want a juice?"

② Ask a female "Do you have an appointment?"

③ Ask a group "Are you from Egypt?"

④ Ask a female "Where are you going?"

⑤ Ask in a café "Do you have cake?"

③ You?

① أنت عاوز عصير؟
enta Aawiz Aaseer

② أنت عندك ميعاد؟
enti Aandik meeAaad

③ أنتم من مصر؟
entum min musr

④ أنت رايحة فين؟
enti raayнa fayn

⑤ أنتم عندكم تورتة؟
entum Aandukum torta

④ Tickets (4 minutes)

You're buying tickets at a train station. Follow the conversation, replying in Arabic following the numbered English prompts.

sabaaн il-khayr, ayy khidma?
① Two tickets to Aswan, please.
dhihaab wi-aawda?
② Yes. Round-trip, please.
tisaeen ginayh, min faдlak
③ What time is the train?
is-saaa khamsa wi-nuss
④ Do we have to reserve seats?
laa. mish muhimm
⑤ Thank you. Goodbye.

④ Tickets

① تذكرتين لأسوان، من فضلك.
tazkartayn l-aswaan, min faдlik

② أيوه، ذهاب وعودة من فضلك.
aywah. dhahaab w-Aawda, min faдlik

③ القطار الساعة كام؟
il-'aтr is-saAaa kaam

④ لازم نحجز كراسي؟
laazim niнgiz karaasi

⑤ شكرا. مع السلامة.
shukran. maAasalaama

Hawl il-madeena
About town

1 Warm up (1 minute)

Ask "How do you get to the museum?" (pp.42-3)

Say "I want to take the metro" and "I'm not taking a taxi." (pp.40-1)

Note that the word **kubree** (bridge) is used widely in Egypt, but **jisr** is also common in other parts of the Arab world. Be careful, too, not to confuse **mektaba** (bookstore or library) and **mektab** (office)—the only difference is the final **a** sound.

2 Match and repeat (4 minutes)

Match the numbered locations to the words in the panel.

❶ كوبري
   kubree

❷ برج
   borg

❸ دار الأوبرا
   daar il-obra

❹ ميدان
   meedaan

❺ مسجد
   masgid

❻ متحف
   methaf

❼ سوق
   soo'

3 Words to remember (4 minutes)

Familiarize yourself with these words and test yourself using the cover flap.

محطة بنزين *maнaттit benzeen*	gas station
مكتب سياحة *mektab siyaaнa*	tourist office
مكتبة *mektaba*	library/ bookstore
وسط البلد *wusт il-balad*	town center

❶ bridge

❷ tower

❹ square

opera ❸ house

❺ mosque

Conversational tip The common expressions *feeh* (*there is/are*) and *ma feesh* (*there isn't/aren't*) will be understood throughout the Arabic-speaking world, but in some dialects of Arabic *ma feesh* is pronounced *ma fee*, without the final *sh* sound. Likewise, *ma ʌandeesh* (*I don't have*) and *ma ʌandinaash* (*we don't have*) can be pronounced *ma ʌandee* and *ma ʌandinaa*, again without the final *sh* sound.

4 **Useful phrases** (4 minutes)

Practice these phrases and then test yourself using the cover flap.

Is there a gas station near here?	فيه محطة بنزين قريبة من هنا؟	
	feeh maнaттit benzeen urayyiba min hina	
(Is it) far from here?	بعيد من هنا؟	
	biʌeed min hina	
There is a market next to the bridge.	فيه سوق جنب الكوبري.	
	feeh soo' ganb il-kubree	

المسجد في وسط البلد.
il-masgid fi wusт il-balad
The mosque is in the town center.

5 **Put into practice** (2 minutes)

Join in this conversation. Read the Arabic on the left and follow the instructions to make your reply. Then test yourself using the cover flap.

أي خدمة؟   فيه مكتبة قريبة من هنا؟
ayyi khidma   *feeh mektaba urayyiba min hina*
Can I help you?
Ask: Is there a bookstore near here?

أيوه، جنب المتحف.   بعيد من هنا؟
aywah, ganb il-metнaf   *biʌeed min hina*
Yes, next to the museum.
Ask: Is it far from here?

⑥ museum

شكرا. لا، هناك.
laa, hinaak   *shukran*
No, over there.
Say: Thank you.

⑦ market

Il-ittigaahaat
Directions

1 **Warm up** (1 minute)

How do you ask "How far is it?" (pp.42-3)

Say "We're taking the bus." (pp.40-1)

Ask a group of people "Where are you going?" (pp.40-1)

When finding your way around a town or city you are not familiar with, it always helps to be able to ask for directions. The smaller streets may not always be well known, so it is a good idea to find out what the local landmarks are, such as markets, stores, or important buildings.

2 **Useful phrases** (4 minutes)

Learn these phrases and then test yourself.

خذ شمال/يمين. *khud shimaal/ yimeen*	Turn left/right. (talking to a male)
خذي شمال/يمين. *khudee shimaal/ yimeen*	Turn left/right. (talking to a female)
على طول *ʌala ʈool*	straight ahead
ازاي أوصل البازار؟ *izzay awsal il-bazaar*	How do I get to the bazaar?
أول يمين *awwil yimeen*	first right
ثاني شمال *taanee shimaal*	second left

تمثال
timsaal
statue

شارع رئيسي
shaareʌ rayeesee
main street

3 **In conversation** (4 minutes)

فيه مطعم قريب؟
feeh maʈaam uraayyib
Is there a restaurant nearby?

أيوه، جنب المحطة.
aywah. ganb il-maнaʈʈa
Yes, near the station.

ازاي أوصل المحطة؟
izzay awsal il-maнaʈʈa
How do I get to the station?

4 Words to remember (4 minutes)

أنا تهت!
ena tuht
I'm lost!

Familiarize yourself with these words and test yourself using the flap.

junction	تقاطع	*taqaatuʌ*
corner	ناصية	*nasya*
street	شارع	*shaareʌ*
the end of the street	آخر الشارع	*aakhir ish-shaareʌ*
map	خريطة	*khareeтa*
at	عند	*ʌand*
in front of	قدام	*uddaam*

عمارة
ʌimaara
apartment block

احنا فين؟
iнna fayn
Where are we?

5 Say it (2 minutes)

Turn right at the corner. (to a male)

Turn left in front of the museum. (to a female)

How do I get to the restaurant?

خذي شمال عند الإشارة.
khudee shimaal ʌand il-ishaara
Turn left at the traffic lights.

المسافة قد إيه؟
il-misaafa adda eh
How far is it?

خمس دقائق مشي.
khamas da'aayi mash-yuh
A five-minute walk.

1 **Warm up** (1 minute)

Say the days of the week in Arabic. (pp.28-9)

How do you say "six o'clock"? (pp.30-1)

Ask "What time is it?" (pp.30-1)

Ziyaarit il-maAaalim
Sightseeing

While many government offices are closed on Friday, the main tourist sites are open every day. The smaller ones often have shorter opening hours on Fridays. It is always worth checking the times of opening before your visit.

2 **Words to remember** (4 minutes)

Familiarize yourself with these words and test yourself using the flap.

دليل سياحي *daleel siyaaнi*	guidebook
تذاكر دخول *tazaakir dukhool*	entrance tickets
مواعيد الزيارة *mawaАeed iz-ziyaara*	opening times
أجازة رسمية *agaaza rasmeyya*	public holiday
دخول مجاني *dukhool maggaani*	free entrance

جولة مع دليل
gawla maA daleel
guided tour

Cultural tip
You may be offered the services of a guide at tourist sites—sometimes this is optional, but sometimes a guided tour is part of the ticket. You should tip the guide at the end of the tour.

3 **In conversation** (3 minutes)

بتفتحوا بعد الظهر؟
bi-tiftaнoo baАd iD-Duhr

Do you open in the afternoon?

أيوه، بس بنقفل الساعة خمسة.
aywah, bass bi-ni'fil is-saaАa khamsa

Yes, but we close at five o'clock.

فيه تسهيلات للمعاقين؟
feeh tas-heelaat lil-muАaqeen

Are there facilities for the disabled?

4 Useful phrases (3 minutes)

Learn these phrases and then test yourself using the cover flap.

What time do you open/close?

بتفتحوا/بتقفلوا الساعة كام؟
bi-tiftaʜoo/bi-ti'filoo is-saaʌa kaam

Where are the restrooms?

فين الحمامات؟
fayn il-ʜammaamaat

Are there facilities for the disabled?

فيه تسهيلات للمعاقين؟
feeh tas-heelaat lil-muʌaqeen

5 Put into practice (4 minutes)

Cover the text on the right and complete the dialog in Arabic.

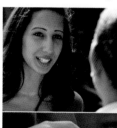

آسف، المتحف مقفول.
aasif. il-metʜaf ma'fool
Sorry. The museum is closed.

Ask: Do you open on Tuesdays?

بتفتحوا يوم الثلاثاء؟
bi-tiftaʜoo yohm it-talaat

أيوه، بس بنقفل بدري.
aywah, bass bi-ni'fil badree
Yes, but we close early.

Ask: At what time?

الساعة كام؟
is-saaʌa kaam

أيوه، فيه أسانسير هناك.
aywah, feeh asanseer hinaak

Yes, there's an elevator over there.

شكرا. عاوزة تذكرتين دخول.
shukran. ʌawza tazkirtayn dukhool

Thank you. I want two entrance tickets.

اتفضلي. الدليل السياحي ده مجاني.
ittfaooalee. id-daleel is-siyaaʜi dah maggaani

Here you are. This guidebook is free.

Fil-maTaar
At the airport

1 Warm up (1 minute)

Say "half past one."
(pp.30-1)

What's the Arabic for
"ticket," "two tickets," and
"three tickets"? (pp.38-9)

Say "I am going
to Aswan." (pp.40-1)

Although airports are generally an international
environment, it is often useful to be able to ask
your way around the terminal in Arabic. It's a
good idea to make sure you have some small
change when you arrive at the airport; you may
need to pay for a luggage cart or tip a porter.

2 Words to remember (4 minutes)

Familiarize yourself with these words and test yourself using the flap.

التسجيل *it-tasgeel*	check-in
مغادرة *mughaadra*	departures
وصول *wusool*	arrivals
جمارك *gamaarik*	customs
رحلة *riHla*	flight
صالة *saala*	terminal
بوابة *bawwaaba*	gate

الرحلة من أي بوابة؟
ir-riHla min ayyi bawwaaba
Which gate does the flight leave from?

3 Useful phrases (3 minutes)

Learn these phrases and then test yourself using the cover flap.

رحلة أسوان في ميعادها؟
*riHlit aswaan fi
miAaad-ha*

Is the flight to
Aswan on time?

مش لاقي شنطي.
mish laa'ee shonaTee

I can't find
my luggage.

4 Put into practice (3 minutes)

Join in this conversation. Read the Arabic on the left and follow the instructions to make your reply. Then test yourself by concealing the answers using the cover flap.

رحلة الغرقة في ميعادها؟
riHlit il-gharda'a fi miAaad-ha

أي خدمة؟
ayyi khidma
Can I help you?

Ask: Is the flight to Hurghada on time?

الرحلة من أي بوابة؟
ir-riHla min ayyi bawwaaba

أيوه يا فندم.
aywah yaa fendim
Yes sir.

Ask: Which gate does the flight leave from?

Gates ↑ البوابات
15 - 50
↑ 15,17   16,18 ↑

5 Match and repeat (4 minutes)

Match the numbered items to the Arabic words in the panel.

1 كارت صعود
kart suAood

2 تذكرة
tazkara

3 جواز السفر
gawaaz is-safar

4 شنطة
shanTa

5 تروللي
trollee

boarding pass **1**

ticket **2**

passport **3**

4 suitcase   **5** cart

Read it The sign below reads *maTaar* (airport). It is written (from right to left): م (m), ط (T), ا (aa), ر (r). Notice that the first *a* is not written (see page 25 for more details on vowels in Arabic script).

مطار

RaagiA wi karrar
Review and repeat

il-agweba
Answers Cover with flap

1 Places

❶ متحف
metHaf

❷ ميدان
midaan

❸ كوبري
kubree

❹ سوق
sooq

❺ برج
borg

❻ مسجد
masgid

❼ دار الأوبرا
daar il-obra

1 Places (4 minutes)

Name the numbered places in Arabic.

❶ museum   **❷** square   **❸** bridge

❹ market   **❺** tower   **❻** mosque

❼ opera house

2 Car parts

❶ بربريز
barabreez

❷ إشارة
ishaara

❸ كبوت
kabboot

❹ عجلة
Aagala

❺ باب
baab

❻ اكسضام
iksiDaam

2 Car parts (3 minutes)

Name these car parts in Arabic.

❶ windshield

❹ tire   **❺** door

3 Questions (4 minutes)

Ask the questions that match these answers.

❶ *ena raayih il-ahraam*

❷ *bi-ni'fil is-saaʌa arbaʌa*

❸ *iʜna ʌawzeen shaay*

❹ *laa. mʌandeesh awlaad*

❺ *khamas da'aayi mash-yuh*

3 Questions

❶ (أنت) رايح فين؟
(enta) raayiʜ fayn

❷ بتقفلوا الساعة كام؟
bi-ti'filoo is-saaʌa kaam

❸ (أنتم) عاوزين إيه؟
(entum) ʌawzeen eh

❹ عندك أولاد؟
ʌandak awlaad

❺ المسافة قد إيه؟
il-misaafa adda eh

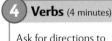

❷ turn signal

❸ hood

❻ bumper

4 Verbs (4 minutes)

Ask for directions to each of these places in Arabic.

❶ the museum

❷ the tower

❸ the market

❹ the mosque

❺ the bazaar

4 Verbs

❶ إزاي أوصل المتحف؟
izzay awsal il-metʜaf

❷ إزاي أوصل البرج؟
izzay awsal il-borg

❸ إزاي أوصل السوق؟
izzay awsal is-sooq

❹ إزاي أوصل المسجد؟
izzay awsal il-masgid

❺ إزاي أوصل البازار؟
izzay awsal il-bazaar

Hagz ghurfa
Booking a room

1 Warm up (1 minute)

Ask "Can I pay by card?" (pp.38-9)

Ask "How much is that?" (pp.18-19)

Ask "Do you have any children?" (to a female) (pp.10-11)

Accommodation for visitors in Arabic-speaking countries ranges from luxury hotels and upscale holiday complexes to small, family-run guest houses. Staff on the front desk of larger hotels usually speak good English, but other staff and owners of small hotels may not.

2 Useful phrases (3 minutes)

Practice these phrases and then test yourself by concealing the Arabic on the left using the cover flap.

شامل الفطور؟
shaamil il-fuтoor

Is breakfast included?

فيه تكييف هواء؟
feeh takeef hawa

Is there air-conditioning?

فيه خدمة غرف؟
feeh khidmit ghuraf

Is there room service?

المغادرة الساعة كام؟
il-mughaadra is-saaаa kaam

What time is check-out?

3 In conversation (5 minutes)

فيه غرف فاضية؟
feeh ghuraf faбya

Do you have any vacant rooms?

أيوه، فيه غرفة لشخصين؟
aywah. feeh ghurfa li-shakhsayn

Yes, there's a double room.

فيه سرير أطفال؟
feeh sireer aтfaal

Is there a cot?

4 **Words to remember** (4 minutes)

Familiarize yourself with these words and test yourself by concealing the Arabic on the right using the cover flap.

room	غرفة	*ghurfa*
single room	غرفة لشخص	*ghurfa li-shakhs*
double room	غرفة لشخصين	*ghurfa li-shakhsayn*
bathroom	حمام	*наmmaam*
balcony	بلكونة	*balkohna*
shower	دش	*dush*
breakfast	فطور	*fuтoor*
key	مفتاح	*moftaaн*

فيه بلكونة؟
feeh balkohna
Is there a balcony?

5 **Say it** (2 minutes)

Do you have a single room, please?

Six nights.

Is dinner included?

Conversational tip Some Arabic words can be made plural by adding one of two endings, *-aat* or *-een*, as in *наmmaam/наmmaamaat* (bathroom/bathrooms) or *muwazzaf/muwazzafeen* (employee/employees). However, many other plurals are made by altering the vowel sounds within a word, as occurs in English with *goose/geese* or *mouse/mice*. Examples of this type of plural include *layla/leyaalee* (night/nights), *ghurfa/ghuraf* (room/rooms), and *тifl/aтfaal* (child/children). You will need to learn these plurals individually.

أيوه، فيه. عاوزين كام ليلة؟
aywah, feeh. ааwzeen kaam layla

Yes, there is. How many nights do you want?

ثلاث ليالي.
talat leyaalee

Three nights.

ماشي. اتفضلوا المفتاح.
maashi. ittafaDDaloo il-moftaaн

That's fine. Here's the key.

1 Warm up (1 minute)

Say "Is/Are there...?"
and "There isn't/aren't..."
(pp.48-9)

What does "*ayyi khidma?*" mean?
(pp.48-9)

Fil-fundu'
In the hotel

Aawiz/Aawza/Aawzeen (m/f/pl) meaning *want*
can also be used to mean *need*. Arabic doesn't have
an equivalent of the English *a, an,* or *some*. So *I need
a blanket* is (**ena**) **Aawiz/Aawza baтaneyya** (literally
need blanket) and *we need some towels* is (**iнna**)
Aawzeen fuwat (*need towels*).

2 Match and repeat (6 minutes)

Match the numbered items in this hotel bedroom with the Arabic text in the panel
and test yourself using the cover flap.

❶ تليفزيون
tileefizyon

❷ كرسي
kursee

❸ روب حمام
rohb нammaam

❹ ستاير
sataayir

❺ نور
noor

❻ شبشب
shibshib

❼ فوطة
fooтa

❽ سرير
sireer

❾ مخدة
makhadda

❶ television

❷ chair

curtains ❹

light ❺

❸ bathrobe

❼ towel ❽ bed

❻ slippers

pillow ❾

Cultural tip In a double room in an Egyptian hotel, you may find one long pillow
instead of two individual ones on the bed. You may also see an arrow on the floor or
on a piece of furniture. This points towards Mecca, the direction Muslims face to pray.
Toilets usually include a small cleansing shower,
sometimes inside the bowl itself, with an accessible
tap to control the flow.

3 Useful phrases (5 minutes)

Practice these phrases and then test yourself using the cover flap.

The room is very cold/hot.

الغرفة برد/حر جدا.
il-ghurfa bard/Harr giddan

There are no towels.

مافيش فوط.
ma feesh fuwaτ

We need some soap.

عاوزين صابون.
Aawzeen saboon

The shower doesn't work.

الدش مش شغال.
id-dush mish shagh-ghaal

The elevator is out of order.

الأسانسير عطلان.
il-asanseer Aaτlaan

4 Put into practice (3 minutes)

Practice these phrases and then complete the dialogue in Arabic.

أي خدمة؟
ayyi khidma
Can I help you?

Say: I need a pillow.

عاوزة مخدة.
Aawza makhadda

حابعتها حالا.
Habaat-ha Haalan
I'll send one straight away.

Say: And the television is out of order.

والتليفزيون عطلان.
wal-tileefizyon Aaτlaan

1 **Warm up** (1 minute)

Ask "Can I?"
(pp.34–5)

Say "The elevator is out of order." (pp.60-1)

Say "We need soap." (pp.60-1)

Aalal markib
On the boat

Boat trips of all kinds are popular with tourists in the Middle East, whether a diving or fishing excursion in the Red Sea, a serene and spectacular float down the Nile in a traditional faluka, or a luxurious sightseeing cruise in a "floating hotel."

2 **Words to remember** (4 minutes)

Learn these words and then test yourself by concealing the Arabic with the cover flap.

مركب *markib*	boat
يخت *yakht*	yacht
مركب غطس *markib ghaтs*	dive boat
مركب صيد *markib sayd*	fishing boat
لنش *lansh*	motorboat/ launch

ممكن نأجر مركب؟
mumkin niaggar markib
Can we rent a boat?

فلوكة
filooka
faluka

3 **In conversation** (5 minutes)

عاوزين نحجز رحلة على النيل.
ʌawzeen niнgiz riнla ʌalan-neel

We want to book a trip on the Nile.

أنا عندي أحسن فلوكة في النيل كله.
ena ʌandee aнsan filooka fin-neel kulluh

I have the best faluka on the whole Nile.

ماشي. الرحلة كام ساعة؟
maashi. ir-riнla kaam saaʌa

OK. How many hours is the trip?

4 Words and phrases to remember (3 minutes)

Learn these words and phrases and then test yourself using the cover flap.

5 Say it (2 minutes)

Can we rent diving gear?

I need a fishing rod.

How much is the trip for children?

lifejacket	سترة النجاة	sutrit in-nagaah
diving gear	عدة الغطس	Aiddit il-ghaTs
fishing gear	عدة الصيد	Aiddit is-sayd
fishing rod	سنارة	sinnaara
bait	طعم	TuAm
Can we rent equipment?	ممكن نأجر عدة؟	mumkin ni'aggar Aidda
I'm a beginner.	أنا مبتدئ.	ena mubtadi'
I can't swim.	ماعرفش أعوم.	maAarafsh aAoom
I'm an experienced swimmer.	أنا سباح ماهر.	ena sabbaaн maahir
Is fishing allowed here?	الصيد مسموح هنا؟	is-sayd masmooн hina
Is it suitable for children?	دي مناسبة للأطفال؟	dee munaasba lil-aTfaal

شراع
shiraaA
sail

عبارة
Aabbaara
ferry

ممكن ساعتين أو ثلاث ساعات.

mumkin saaAatayn ow talaat saaAaat

It can be two or three hours.

بكام الرحلة دي لشخصين؟

bikaam ir-riнla dee li-shakhsayn

How much is this trip for two people?

ثلاثين جنيه النفر.

talateen ginayh in-nafar

Thirty pounds per person.

1 Warm up (1 minute)

How do you say
"the room is hot"?
(pp.60-1)

What is the Arabic
for "bed," "towel,"
and "pillow"? (pp.60-1)

Il-wasf
Descriptions

Adjectives are descriptive words. In Arabic an
adjective usually follows the thing it describes and
is in the same gender, as in *sireer kibeer* (a large bed,
masculine/singular) or *ghurfa kibeera* (a large room,
feminine/singular); but *il-ghurfa kibeera* (<u>the</u> room
[is] large).

2 Words to remember (7 minutes)

Most adjectives change depending on whether the thing described is masculine
or feminine. Generally, the feminine form of an adjective ends in *-a*. Be aware
that this addition sometimes affects the pronunciation; the preceding vowel
sounds may be contracted.

سخن/-ة	hot
sukhn/sukhna	
بارد/-ة	cold
baarid/baarda	
كبير/-ة	big/large
kibeer/kibeera	
صغير/-ة	small
sughayyar/sughayyara	
دوشة	noisy
dawsha (m/f)	
هادي/-ة	quiet
haadi/haadya	
جديد/-ة	new
gideed/gideeda	
قديم/-ة	old
adeem/adeema	
كويس/-ة	nice/good
kwayyis/kwayyisa	

الجو كويس.
ig-gaw kwayyis
The weather is nice.

Read it The feminine ending *-a* is written in
Arabic script as a circle with two dots above: ة.
This is called **taa marbooта** (tied-up T) because
it can also be pronounced *-t* or *-it* when placed
in certain word combinations. For example,
غرفة (*ghurfa*, room), but غرفة الأولاد (*ghurfit
il-awlaad*, the children's room).

3 Useful phrases (4 minutes)

Learn these phrases. Note that you can qualify a description by using **giddan** (*very*) or **shwayya** (*a little*) after the adjective.

	The coffee is cold.	القهوة باردة. *il-ahwa baarda*
	My room is very noisy.	غرفتي دوشة جدا. *ghurfitee dawsha giddan*
	The car is a little small.	السيارة صغيرة شوية. *is-sayyaara sughayyara shwayya*
	I need a new pillow.	عاوز مخدة جديدة. ʌawiz makhadda gideeda

4 Put into practice (3 minutes)

Join in this conversation. Cover up the text on the right and complete the dialog in Arabic. Check and repeat if necessary.

دي غرفتكم.
dee ghurfitkum
This is your room.
Say: The view is very beautiful.

المنظر جميل جدا.
il-manzar gameel giddan

الحمام هناك.
il-нammaam hinaak
The bathroom is over there.
Say: It's a little small.

ده صغير شوية.
dah sughayyar shwayya

آسف، الفندق مليان.
aasif. il-fundu' malyaan
I'm sorry. The hotel is full.
Say: It's not important.

مش مهم.
mish muhimm

RaagiA wi karrar
Review and repeat

il-agweba
Answers Cover with flap

1 Descriptions

❶ باردة
baarda

❷ كبير
kibeer

❸ سخنة
sukhna

❹ جميل
gameel

❺ هادية
haadya

1 Descriptions (3 minutes)

Put the word in brackets into Arabic. Use the correct masculine or feminine form.

❶ il-ghurfa _____ (cold)

❷ il Hammaam _____ (large) giddan

❸ il-mayya _____ (hot) shwayya

❹ il-baHr _____ (beautiful)

❺ ena Aawiz ghurfa _____ (quiet)

2 In the hotel

❶ تليفزيون
tileefizyon

❷ كرسي
kursee

❸ روب حمام
rohb Hammaam

❹ ستاير
sataayir

❺ نور
noor

❻ شبشب
shibshib

❼ فوطة
fooTa

❽ سرير
sireer

❾ مخدة
makhadda

2 In the hotel (3 minutes)

Name these items you might find in a hotel room.

❶ television ❷ chair ❹ curtains
❸ bathrobe
❼ towel ❽ bed
❻ slippers

3 **At the hotel** (4 minutes)

You are booking a room in a hotel. Follow the conversation, replying in Arabic where you can see the English prompts.

ayyi khidma?
1 Do you have any vacant rooms?

feeh ghurfa li-shakhs
2 Is there air-conditioning?

aywa. ʌawiz kaam layla?
3 Three nights.

maashi
4 Is breakfast included?

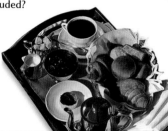

3 **At the hotel**

1 فيه غرف فاضية؟
feeh ghuraf faɒya

2 فيه تكييف هواء؟
feeh takeef hawa

3 ثلاث ليالي.
talat leyaalee

4 شامل الفطور؟
shaamil il-fuтoor

4 **Negatives** (5 minutes)

Make these sentences negative using **mish** (not).

1 *il-ghurfa haadya*

2 *il-ahwa sukhna*

3 *iнna min muṣr*

4 *il-maтʌam ganb il-maнaттa*

5 *huwa ʌawiz makhadda gideeda*

5 light

9 pillow

4 **Negatives**

1 الغرفة مش هادية.
il-ghurfa mish haadya

2 القهوة مش سخنة.
il-ahwa mish sukhna

3 احنا مش من مصر.
iнna mish min muṣr

4 المطعم مش جنب المحطة.
il-maтʌam mish ganb il-maнaттa

5 هو مش عاوز مخدة جديدة.
huwa mish ʌawiz makhadda gideeda

Il-maHallaat
Stores

1 **Warm up** (1 minute)

Ask "How do I get to the station?" (pp.50-1)

Say "Turn left at the traffic lights" and "The station is near the museum." (pp.50-1)

Small, traditional stores and stalls are common in Middle Eastern towns and cities. You will also find local markets and street vendors everywhere selling fresh produce and sometimes drinks and snacks. However, there are growing numbers of supermarkets and out-of-town shopping centers.

2 **Match and repeat** (5 minutes)

Match the stores numbered 1 to 9 to the Arabic in the panel. Then test yourself using the cover flap.

❶ مخبز
makhbaz

❷ حلواني
Halawaanee

❸ كشك سجاير
koshk sagaayir

❹ جزار
gazzaar

❺ محل عصير
maHall Aaseer

❻ مكتبة
mektaba

❼ سمّاك
sammaak

❽ جواهرجي
gawahirgee

❾ بنك
bank

❶ bakery

❷ pastry shop

❹ butcher

❺ juice bar

❼ fish counter

❽ jeweler

Cultural tip A common sight on the streets of Cairo is the *makwagee* (*ironing shop*). For a small cost, you can have all your ironing done and delivered to you within a few hours. Other shops and services often available include the *maHaal gulood* (*leather shop*), which does shoe repairs, and the *labbaan* (*milkman*), who sells and delivers fresh milk, yogurt, and milk-based puddings.

3 **Words to remember** (4 minutes)

محل الورد فين؟
maHaal il-ward fayn
Where is the florist?

Familiarize yourself with these words and test yourself using the flap.

grocery store	بقال	*ba'aal*
antique store	محل انتيكات	*maHall anteekaat*
hairdresser (women's)	كوافير	*kwaafeer*
produce stand	خضري	*khudaree*
post office	مكتب البريد	*mektab il-bareed*
shoe store	محل جزم	*maHall gizam*
dry cleaner	محل تنظيف	*maHall tanDeef*

❸ cigarette kiosk

❻ bookstore

❾ bank

4 **Useful phrases** (3 minutes)

Familiarize yourself with these phrases and then test yourself using the cover flap.

Where is the hairdresser?	الكوافير فين؟	*il-kwaafeer fayn*
Where do I pay?	أدفع فين؟	*adfaA fayn*
I'm just looking, thank you.	بأخذ فكرة بس، شكرا.	*bakhud fikra bass, shukran*
Do you sell SIM cards?	بتبيعوا سمكارت؟	*bitbeeAoo sim-kart*
May I have two of those?	ممكن اثنين من دول؟	*mumkin itnayn min dool*
Can you order that for me?	ممكن تجهزلي طلبي؟	*mumkin tigahhizlee Talabee*

5 **Say it** (2 minutes)

Where is the bank?

Do you sell cheese?

May I have five of those?

1 **Warm up** (1 minute)

What is Arabic for 40, 56, 77, 82, and 94? (pp.10-11, pp.30-1)

Say "I need a big room." (pp.64-5)

Ask "Do you have a small car?" (pp.58-9, pp.64-5)

Fil-bazaar
In the bazaar

Shopping in the traditional bazaars of the Arab world is an experience not to be missed. As well as the usual tourist souvenirs, bazaars often have areas dedicated to particular local crafts or products, such as perfumes, spices, rugs, jewelry, leather, and furniture.

2 **Match and repeat** (4 minutes)

Match the numbered items in this scene with the text in the panel.

1 نحاس
naHaas

2 ورق بردي
waraq bardee

3 قطن
uтn

4 حرير
Hareer

5 فضة
faDDa

6 جلابية
galabeyya

7 صدف
sadaf

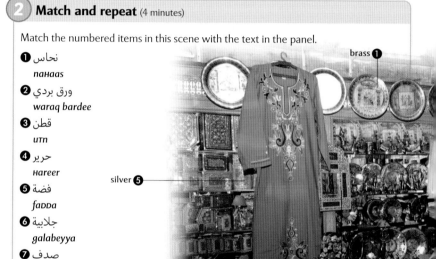

brass **1**

silver **5**

robe **6**

7 mother-of-pearl

3 **In conversation** (5 minutes)

عاوزة جلابية قطن.
Aawza galabeyya uтn
I want a cotton galabeyya.

عندي دي. جميلة!
Aandee dee. gameela
I have this one. Beautiful!

أيوه، جميلة. بكام دي؟
aywah, gameela. bi-kaam dee
Yes, it's beautiful. How much is it?

Cultural tip Bartering is an essential part of the shopping experience in a bazaar. Stall holders expect you to haggle, but it is better to keep the negotiation light-hearted rather than turning it into a battle of wills. You will always strike a better bargain if you are prepared to buy more than one item from the same stall.

② papyrus

③ cotton

④ silk

4 **Useful phrases** (4 minutes)

Learn these phrases. Then cover up the answers on the right. Read the English under the pictures and say the phrase in Arabic as shown on the right.

Anything else, madam?

أي خدمة ثانية يا مدام؟
ayyi khidma tanya yaa madaam

That's very expensive.

دي غالية جدا.
dee ghalya giddan

Is that your final price?

ده آخر كلام؟
dah aakhir kalaam

5 **Say it** (1 minute)

I want a silk galabeyya.

One hundred and ninety is fair.

That's expensive.

مية وثمانين بس.
mia wi-tamaneen bass
Only 180.

لا، دي غالية. مية وخمسين كويس.
laa, dee ghalya. mia wi-khaseen kwayyis
No, that's expensive. 150 is fair.

ماشي. مية وسبعين علشانك انت بس.
maashi. mia wi-sabaAeen Aalashaanik enti bass
OK. 170 just for you.

Fil-subermarkit
At the supermarket

Warm up (1 minute)

What are these items you could buy in a supermarket? (pp.24-5)

samak
gibna
makarona
laнma
khuⅮaar
firaakh

Until relatively recently, self-service shopping was not common in the Arabic-speaking world. However, increasing numbers of supermarkets are now appearing in the larger towns and resorts. These often have their own bakery, butcher, and cheese counter, and may also serve prepared meals.

Match and repeat (5 minutes)

Look at the numbered product categories and match them to the Arabic words in the panel on the left.

❶ منتجات منزلية
muntagaat manzileyya

❷ فواكه
fawaakih

❸ مشروبات
mashroobaat

❹ وجبات جاهزة
wagbaat gahza

❺ منتجات تجميل
muntagaat tagmeel

❻ منتجات ألبان
muntagaat albaan

❼ خضار
khudaar

❽ منتجات مجمدة
muntagaat mugammada

household ❶ products

fruit ❷

drinks ❸

ready meals ❹

vegetables ❼   frozen foods ❽

Conversational tip The Arabic words for everyday items such as basic foods can vary depending on the dialect of the region. For example, in Egypt *bread* is generally called **Ɑaysh** and *milk* is called **laban**, but in some other parts of the Arabic-speaking world, the words **khubz** and **нaleeb** are more common.

3 **Useful phrases** (3 minutes)

Learn these phrases and then test yourself using the cover flap.

May I have a bag, please? | مكن كيس من فضلك؟
mumkin kees min faɒlak

Where are the drinks? | المشروبات فين؟
il-mashroobaat fayn

Where do I pay? | أدفع فين؟
adfaʌ fayn

Is this card accepted? | الكارت ده مقبول؟
il-kart dah ma'bool

⑤ beauty products

⑥ dairy products

4 **Words to remember** (4 minutes)

Learn these words and then test yourself using the cover flap.

bread	عيش *ʌaysh*
milk	لبن *laban*
butter	زبدة *zibda*
salt	ملح *malн*
pepper	فلفل *filfil*
laundry detergent	مسحوق غسيل *mas-нooq ghaseel*
toilet paper	ورق تواليت *wara' twaalett*
diapers	حفاضات *нafaaɒaat*

5 **Say it** (2 minutes)

Where are the dairy products?

May I have some ham, please?

Where are the frozen foods?

Il-malaabis wil-gizam
Clothes and shoes

1 Warm up (1 minute)

Ask "Can I have...?"
(pp.22-3)

Ask "Do you have...?"
(pp.12-13)

Say "38," "42," and "46."
(pp.10-11, pp.30-1)

Say "big" and "small."
(pp.64-5)

Clothes and shoes are measured in metric sizes. Given time you can have items tailor made for a reasonable price. Clothes specifically for ladies are described as **ңareemee**—from the old word **ңareem**, meaning *women*.

2 Match and repeat (4 minutes)

Match the numbered items of clothing to the Arabic words in the panel on the left. Test yourself using the cover flap.

❶ قميص
amees

❷ كرافتة
kravatta

❸ جاكتة
jaketta

❹ جيب
gayb

❺ كم
komm

❻ بنطلون
bantalon

❼ جيبة
jeeba

❽ جزمة
gazma

shirt **❶**

tie **❷**

jacket **❸**

pocket **❹**

sleeve **❺**

pants **❻**

Cultural tip Words for Western clothing vary between regions: *jeeba* (skirt) can also be *gunella* or *tannoora*. Traditional garments vary in style and have different names in different areas. Such items include the Egyptian *galabeyya* robe, the Palestinian *kufeyya* scarf, and the long, white *dishdasha* or *thawb* worn in the Gulf.

3 **Useful phrases** (5 minutes)

Practice these phrases and then test yourself using the cover flap.

Is there a larger size? فيه مقاس أكبر؟

feeh mi'aas akbar

No, that's not suitable. لا، ده مش مناسب.

laa, dah mish munaasib

I'll take the pink one. آخذ الوردي.

aakhud il-wardee

4 **Words to remember** (5 minutes)

Most adjectives can be made feminine by adding م (pp.64–5), but the principal colors have a special feminine form.

red (m/f)	أحمر/حمراء *aнmar/Hamra*
white (m/f)	أبيض/بيضاء *abyaɒ/bayɒa*
blue (m/f)	أزرق/زرقاء *azra'/zar'a*
yellow (m/f)	أصفر/صفراء *asfar/safra*
green (m/f)	أخضر/خضراء *akhɒar/khaɒra*
black (m/f)	أسود/سوداء *iswid/sohda*

7 skirt

8 shoes

Read it In Arabic script, 1 and 9 are easily recognizable, but other numbers look quite different. A zero is written as a dot:

• · (0), ١ (1), ٢ (2), ٣ (3), ٤ (4), ٥ (5),
٦ (6), ٧ (7), ٨ (8), ٩ (9).

4015 ٤·١٥

RaagiA wi karrar
Review and repeat

il-agweba
Answers Cover with flap

1 Bazaar

❶ فضة
faDDa

❷ جلابية
galabeyya

❸ نحاس
naHaas

❹ قطن
uTn

❺ حرير
Hareer

1 Bazaar (3 minutes)

Name the numbered items in Arabic.

❶ silver ❷ robe brass ❸ cotton ❹ ❺ silk

2 Description

❶ The shirt is a little expensive.

❷ The room is very small.

❸ We want a large car.

2 Description (2 minutes)

What do these sentences mean?

❶ il-amees ghalee shwayya

❷ il-ghurfa sughayyara giddan

❸ iHna Aawzeen sayyaara kibeera

3 Shops

❶ مخبز
makhbaz

❷ جواهرجي
gawahirgee

❸ مكتبة
mektaba

❹ سمّاك
sammaak

❺ حلواني
Halawaanee

❻ جزار
gazzaar

3 Shops (3 minutes)

Name the numbered shops in Arabic. Then check your answers.

❶ bakery ❷ jeweler ❸ bookstore

❹ fish counter ❺ pastry shop ❻ butcher

4 Supermarket (3 minutes)

What is the Arabic for the numbered product categories?

❶ household products

❷ beauty products

❸ drinks

❹ dairy products

❺ frozen foods

4 Supermarket

❶ منتجات منزلية
muntagaat manzileyya

❷ منتجات تجميل
muntagaat tagmeel

❸ مشروبات
mashroobaat

❹ منتجات ألبان
muntagaat albaan

❺ منتجات مجمدة
muntagaat mugammada

5 Museum (4 minutes)

Follow this conversation, replying in Arabic following the English prompts.

ayyi khidma?
❶ We want five entrance tickets.
mia wi-khamseen, min faɒlak
❷ That's very expensive!
shaamil gawla maʌ dileel
❸ Is there a lift?
aywah. il-asanseer hinaak
❹ OK. Five tickets, please.
ittafaɒɒal
❺ Thank you. Where are the restrooms?

5 Museum

❶ عاوزين خمس تذاكر دخول.
ʌawizeen khamas tadhaakir dukhool

❷ ده غالي جدا!
dah ghaali giddan

❸ فيه أسانسير؟
feeh asanseer

❹ ماشي. خمس تذاكر من فضلك.
maashi. khamas tadhaakir min faɒlak(-ik)

❺ شكرا. فين الحمامات؟
shukran. fayn il-ʜammaamaat

1 **Warm up** (1 minute)

Say "I have a meeting."
(pp.14-15)

What is the Arabic for
the following family
members: sister, brother,
mother, father, son, and
daughter? (pp.10-11)

Ish-shughl
Work

When describing occupations, you don't need the
equivalent of am/are/is or a/an, saying **ena таbbaakh**
(*I [male] am a cook*); **heyya mumarriда** (*she is a nurse*).
When referring to a female, add **-a** to the occupation—
for example, **doktoora** (*female doctor*).

2 **Words to remember: jobs** (7 minutes)

Familiarize yourself with these words and test yourself
using the cover flap.

دكتور *doktoor*	doctor	
دكتور أسنان *doktoor asnaan*	dentist	
ممرض *mumarriд*	nurse	
مدرس *mudarris*	teacher	
محام *muнaami*	lawyer	
محاسب *muнaasib*	accountant	
مصمم *musammim*	designer	
سكرتير *sekertayr*	secretary	
كهربائي *kahrabaa'ee*	electrician	
سباك *sabbaak*	plumber	
طباخ *таbbaakh*	cook/chef	
رجل أعمال/سيدة أعمال *ragul аamaal/* *sayyidit аamaal*	businessman/ businesswoman	

أنا سباك.
ena sabbaak
I'm a plumber.

هي طالبة.
heyya таaliba
She is a student.

3 Put into practice (4 minutes)

Join in this conversation. Read the Arabic on the left and follow the instructions to make your reply. Then test yourself using the flap.

بتشتغل إيه؟ أنا رجل أعمال.
btishtaghil eh *ena ragul ʌamaal*
What's your job?

Say: I'm a businessman.

عندك شركة؟ أيوه، عندي شركة صغيرة.
ʌandak sherika *aywah, ʌandee*
Do you have a company? *sherika sughayyara*

Say: Yes. I have a
small company.

عظيم! وأنت، بتشتغل إيه؟
ʌazeem *w-enta, btishtaghil eh*
Great!

Say: And you, what's
your job?

أنا دكتور. أختي كمان دكتورة.
ena doktoor *ukhtee kamaan doktoora*
I'm a doctor.

Say: My sister is
also a doctor.

4 Words to remember: workplace (3 minutes)

Familiarize yourself with these words and then test yourself.

branch	فرع *farʌ*
department	قسم *qism*
manager	مدير *mudeer*
employee	موظف *muwazzaf*
trainee	تحت التمرين *taнt it-tamreen*

المركز الرئيسي في القاهرة.
il-markaz ir-ra'eesee fil qaahira
Head office is in Cairo.

1 Warm up (1 minute)

Practice different ways of introducing yourself in different situations (pp.8-9). Mention your name, occupation (pp.78-9), and other information you'd like to volunteer.

Il-mektab
The office

Any business or office has its own vocabulary, but there are many words that are useful in most businesses. Arabic computer keyboards show the individual letters (see The Arabic alphabet, pp.155-56) and the software joins the letters as you type.

2 Words to remember (5 minutes)

Familiarize yourself with these words. Read them aloud and try to memorize them. Conceal the Arabic with the cover flap and test yourself.

شاشة *shaasha*	monitor/screen
فار *faar*	mouse
ايميل *email*	email
انترنت *internet*	internet
كلمة المرور *kilmit il-muroor*	password
رسالة صوتية *risaala sohteyya*	voicemail
مفتاح للواي فاي *muftaaн lil-wifi*	Wi-Fi code
ماكينة تصوير *makanit tasweer*	photocopier
أجندة *ajenda*	diary
كارت شخصي *kart shakhsee*	business card
اجتماع *igtimaaл*	meeting
مؤتمر *mu'tamar*	conference

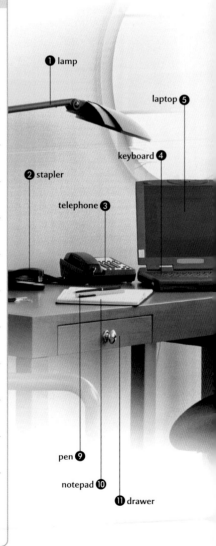

① lamp
laptop ⑤
② stapler
keyboard ④
telephone ③
pen ⑨
notepad ⑩
⑪ drawer

3 Useful phrases (2 minutes)

Learn these phrases and then test yourself using the cover flap.

Can I use the photocopier? ممكن استخدم ماكينة التصوير؟
mumkin astakhdam maakanit it-tasweer

I (m) want to make an appointment. عاوز آخذ ميعاد.
ʌawiz aakhud miʌaad

I (f) want to send an email. عاوز ابعث ايميل.
ʌawiza abʌat email

4 Match and repeat (5 minutes)

6 desk

7 clock

8 printer

Match the numbered items to the Arabic words on the right. Try to memorize them and then test yourself using the cover flap.

1 لمبة
lamba

2 دباسة
dabbaasa

3 تليفون
tilifohn

4 كيبورد
keebord

5 كمبيوتر محمول
kombyootir maнmool

6 مكتب
mektab

7 منبه
menabbih

8 ماكينة طباعة
makanit тabaʌa

9 قلم
alam

10 نوتة
nota

11 درج
dorg

5 Say it (2 minutes)

I have a laptop.

I want to arrange a meeting.

Do you have email?

1 Warm up (1 minute)

Say "library" and "Great!" (pp.48-9, pp.78-9)

Ask "What is your job?" and answer "I'm a teacher." (pp.78-9)

Il-Aalam il-akaadeemee
Academic world

In most Arabic-speaking countries, students are selected for a college degree according to their results in final school exams. Competition for places in faculties such as medicine and engineering is often fierce.

2 Useful phrases (3 minutes)

Practice these phrases and then test yourself using the cover flap.

مجالك إيه؟ *magaalak/-ik eh*	**What is your field?** (m/f)	

| أبحاث في الكيمياء العضوية.
abнaath fil-kimyaa il-ʌuɒwiyya | **Research in biochemistry.** | |

| عندي شهادة في الحقوق.
ʌandee shihaada fil-нuqooq | **I have a degree in law.** |  |

| حالقي محاضرة عن المعمار.
hal'ee muнaɒra ʌan il-miʌmaar | **I'm going to give a lecture on architecture.** |  |

3 In conversation (5 minutes)

أهلاً، أنا بروفيسير هالة شوقي.
ahlan, ena brofeseer haala shawqi

Hello, I'm Professor Hala Shawqi.

من أي جامعة؟
min ayyi gamʌa

From which university?

من جامعة اسكندرية.
min gamʌit iskandareyya

From the University of Alexandria.

4 **Words to remember** (4 minutes)

Familiarize yourself with these words and then test yourself by concealing the Arabic on the right with the cover flap.

عندنا جناح في المعرض التجاري.
Aandina ginaaH fil-maAraD it-tugaaree
We have a stand at the trade fair.

conference	مؤتمر
	mu'tamar
lecture	محاضرة
	muHaDra
trade fair	معرض تجاري
	maAraD tugaaree
lecture hall	قاعة محاضرات
	qaaAit muHaDraat
exhibition	معرض
	maAraD
university lecturer	أستاذ جامعي
	ustaaz gaamAee
professor	بروفيسير
	brofeseer
medicine	طب
	Tibb
science	علوم
	Auloom
arts	آداب
	aadaab
engineering	هندسة
	handasa

5 **Say it** (2 minutes)

Research in medicine.

I have a degree in engineering.

Where's the lecture hall?

مَجالك إيه؟
magaalik eh
What's your field?

أبحاث في هندسة البترول.
abHaath fi handasit il-betrool
Research in
petro-engineering.

عظيم! وأنا كمان.
Aazeem. w-ena kamaan
Great! Me too.

1 **Warm up** (1 minute)

Ask "Can I ...?" (pp.34-5)

Say "I want to send an email." (pp.80-1)

Say "I want to arrange an appointment." (pp.80-1)

Fil-Aamaal
In business

You will make a good impression and receive a more friendly reception if you make the effort to begin your business meetings with a few introductory words in Arabic, even if your vocabulary is limited. After that, everyone will probably be happy to continue the meeting in English.

2 **Words to remember** (6 minutes)

Familiarize yourself with these words and then test yourself by concealing the Arabic with the cover flap.

عميل
Aameel
client

جدول *gadwal*	schedule
تسليم *tasleem*	delivery
دفع *dafA*	payment
ميزانية *mizaaneyya*	budget
سعر *siAr*	price
فاتورة *fatoora*	invoice
عرض *AarD*	proposal
أرباح *arbaaH*	profits
مبيعات *mubeeAaat*	sales

تقرير
taqreer
report

Cultural tip The concept of hospitality extends to business in the Arab world. As a visiting client you can expect to be fed and entertained, and as a supplier you should consider taking gifts and entertaining your business customers when they visit you.

نمضي العقد؟
nimDee il-Aa'd
Shall we sign the contract?

مدير
mudeer
manager

عقد
Aa'd
contract

3 Useful phrases (6 minutes)

Practice these useful business phrases and then test yourself by concealing the Arabic using the cover flap.

ابعث لي العقد من فضلك.
ibAatlee il-Aa'd min faDlak

Please send me
the contract.

اتفقنا على الجدول؟
ittafa'na Aalal gadwal

Have we agreed
the schedule?

ميعاد التسليم امتى؟
miAaad it-tasleem imta

When is the delivery date?

الميزانية كام؟
il-mizaaneyya kaam

How much is the budget?

Read it Many letters of the Arabic alphabet share the same shape and are only distinguished by the number of dots above or below. These dots are an integral part of the letter, just like the dot of the "j" or the cross of the "t". They should not be confused with the optional vowel marks (see pp.25 and 157). Letters that share shapes are:

ب (**b**), ت (**t**), and ث (**th/t**)   د (**d**) and ذ (**dh/z**)

س (**s**) and ش (**sh**)   ر (**r**) and ز (**z**)

ج (**j/g**), ح (**H**), and خ (**kh**)   ص (**s**) and ض (**D**)

ط (**T**) and ظ (**z/D**)   ع (**A**) and غ (**gh**)

4 Say it (2 minutes)

Please send me
the schedule.

Have we agreed
the price?

How much is the invoice?

RaagiA wi karrar
Review and repeat

1   At the office

❶ دباسة
dabbaasa

❷ لمبة
lamba

❸ كمبيوتر محمول
kombyootir маhmool

❹ قلم
alam

❺ منبه
menabbih

❻ نوتة
nota

❼ مكتب
mektab

1   At the office (4 minutes)

Name these items.

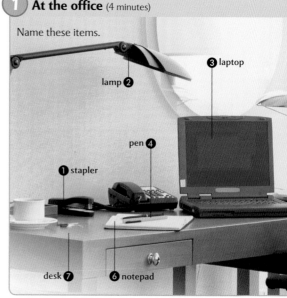

❸ laptop

lamp ❷

pen ❹

❶ stapler

desk ❼   ❻ notepad

2   Jobs

❶ دكتور
doktoor

❷ سباك
sabbaak

❸ طباخ
таbbaakh

❹ محاسب
миhaasib

❺ طالب
таalib

❻ محام
миhaami

2   Jobs (3 minutes)

What are these jobs in Arabic?

❶ doctor

❷ plumber

❸ cook/chef

❹ accountant

❺ student

❻ lawyer

③ **Work** (4 minutes)

Answer these questions following the English prompts.

shughlak eh?
❶ Say: I am a university lecturer.

min ayyi gamʌa?
❷ Say: From the University of London.

magaalak eh?
❸ Say: Research in medicine.

Halqee muнaдra innahaarda
❹ Say: Great! Me too.

❺ clock

③ **Work**

❶ أنا أستاذ جامعي.
ena ustaaz gaamʌee

❷ من جامعة لندن.
min gamʌit london

❸ أبحاث في الطب.
abнaath fiт-тibb

❹ عظيم! وأنا كمان.
ʌazeem. w-ena kamaan

④ **How much?** (4 minutes)

Answer the question with the amount shown in brackets.

❶ *bikaam il-ahwa?*
(8 pounds)

❷ *bikaam il-ghurfa?*
(190 pounds)

❸ *bikaam il-galabeyya?*
(75 pounds)

❹ *bikaam ir-riнla?*
(36 pounds)

④ **How much?**

❶ ٨ جنيه
tamanya ginayh

❷ ١٩٠ جنيه
miya wi-tisʌeen ginayh

❸ ٧٥ جنيه
khamsa wi-sabʌeen ginayh

❹ ٣٦ جنيه
sitta wi-talateen ginayh

1 Warm up (1 minute)

Say "Can I help you?".
(pp.60-1)

Say "I have," "do you
have?" (masculine/
feminine), "he has,"
and "she has."
(pp.14-15)

Fis-saydaleyya
At the pharmacy

The Arabic word for *medicine* is **dawa**. Pharmacists
are qualified to give advice on minor ailments and
sell over-the-counter medicines. You may also be
able to buy strong painkillers and antibiotics from
a pharmacy, but it is always advisable to consult a
doctor before taking such medicines.

2 Match and repeat (3 minutes)

Match the numbered items to the Arabic
words in the panel on the left and test
yourself using the cover flap.

❶ رباط
robaaт

❷ دواء سائل
dawa saayil

❸ نقط
nu'aт

❹ بلاستر
blaaster

❺ حقنة
нu'na

❻ كريم
kreem

❼ حبوب
нuboob

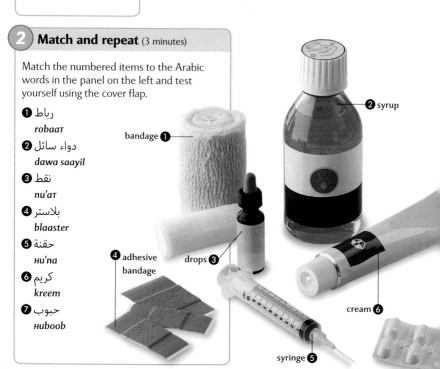

bandage ❶

❷ syrup

❹ adhesive
bandage

drops ❸

cream ❻

syringe ❺

3 In conversation (3 minutes)

صباح الخير.
أي خدمة؟
*sabaaн il-khayr.
ayyi khidma*

Good morning. Can
I help you?

عندي مغص.
Aandee maghas

I have a stomachache.

عندك إسهال؟
Aandak is-haal

Do you have diarrhea?

4 Words to remember (2 minutes)

Familiarize yourself with these words and test yourself using the flap.

عندي صداع.
AAndee sodaaA
I have a headache.

headache	صداع	*sodaaA*
stomachache	مغص	*maghas*
diarrhea	إسهال	*is-haal*
cold	برد	*bard*
cough	كحة	*koннa*
toothache	ألم أسنان	*alam asnaan*

6 Say it (2 minutes)

I have a cold.

Do you have that as a cream?

He has toothache.

5 Useful phrases (4 minutes)

Practice these phrases and then test yourself using the cover flap.

I have sunstroke.	أخذت ضربة شمس.	*akhadt ᴅarbit shams*
Do you have that as drops?	عندكم ده نقط؟	*AAndakum dah nu'at*
I have an allergy to penicillin.	عندي حساسية للبنسلين.	*AAndee ннassaaseyya lil-benesilin*

❼ tablets

لا، بس عندي صداع.
laa, bass AAndee sodaaA
No, but I have a headache.

جرب ده.
garrab dah
Try this.

عندكم ده حبوب؟
AAndukum dah ннuboob
Do you have that as tablets?

1 **Warm up** (1 minute)

Say "I have toothache" and "I have a cough." (pp.88-9)

What's the Arabic for "red," "yellow," and "black" (masculine and feminine forms)? (pp.74-5)

Il-gism
The body

You are most likely to refer to parts of the body in the context of illness—for example, when describing a problem to a doctor. A useful phrase for talking about discomfort is **Aandee alam fi...** (*I have a pain in...*). To ask *What's the matter?* say **maalak?** when talking to a man and **maalik?** to a woman.

2 **Match and repeat: body** (6 minutes)

Match the numbered parts of the body with the list on the left. Test yourself by using the cover flap.

1 رأس
raas

2 رقبة
ra'aba

3 صدر
sidr

4 كوع
kooA

5 بطن
baтn

6 رجل
rigl

7 ركبة
rukba

8 قدم
qadam

9 كتف
kitf

10 ذراع
diraaA

11 يد
yad

head **1**
neck **2**
chest **3**
elbow **4**
stomach **5**
leg **6**
knee **7**
foot **8**

9 shoulder
10 arm
hand **11**

3 Match and repeat: face (3 minutes)

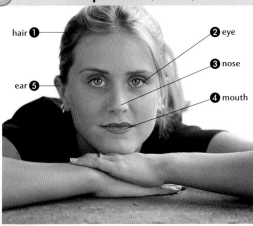

hair **1**

2 eye

3 nose

ear **5**

4 mouth

Match the numbered facial features with the list below.

1 شعر
shaAr

2 عين
Aayn

3 أنف
anf

4 فم
fam

5 أذن
uThun

4 Useful phrases (3 minutes)

Learn these phrases and then test yourself using the cover flap.

	I have a pain in my back.	عندي ألم في ظهري. Aandee alam fi Dahree
	I have a swelling on my arm.	عندي ورم في ذراعي. Aandee waram fi diraaAee
	I don't feel well.	عندي شعور بالتعب. Aandee shuAoor bit-taAb

5 Put into practice (2 minutes)

Join in this conversation and test yourself using the cover flap.

عندي شعور بالتعب.
Aandee shuAoor bit-taAb

مالك؟
maalik
What's the matter?
Say: I don't feel well.

فين الألم؟
fayn il-alam
Where does it hurt?
Say: I have a pain in my shoulder.

عندي ألم في كتفي.
Aandee alam fi kitfee

1 **Warm up** (1 minute)

Say "I have a stomachache." (pp.88-9)

Say "I have an allergy." (pp.88-9)

What is the Arabic for "I'm not British"? (pp.14-15)

Aand id-doktoor
At the doctor

Unless it's an emergency, you should book an appointment with the doctor. You will be expected to pay when you leave, but you can usually reclaim the money if you have medical insurance. Your hotel or a local pharmacy may be able to tell you the names and addresses of doctors in the area.

2 **Useful phrases you may hear** (3 minutes)

Practise these phrases and then test yourself using the cover flap to conceal the Arabic on the left.

بتشتكي من إيه؟ *bitishkee min eh*	What's the problem?
الحالة مش خطرة. *il-Haala mish khaTra*	It's not serious.
لازم نعمل شوية تحاليل. *laazim naAmal shwayyit taHaaleel*	We have to do some tests.
عندك التهاب. *Aandak/-ik iltihaab*	You have (m/f) an infection.
لازم تروح/تروحي المستشفى. *laazim tirooH/tirooHee il-mustashfa*	You must (m/f) go to hospital.

حاكتب لك روشتة.
Haktub lak/lik roshetta
I'm going to write you (m/f) a prescription.

3 **In conversation** (5 minutes)

بتشتكي من إيه؟
bitishkee min eh
What's the problem?

عندي ألم في صدري.
Aandee alam fi sidree
I have a pain in my chest.

اكشف عليك من فضلك.
akshif Aalayki min fadlik
Let me examine you, please.

Cultural tip
Most doctors speak good English, but support staff may not. When telephoning for an appointment, you may need to explain your problem briefly in Arabic to a receptionist or nurse.

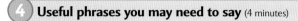

4 **Useful phrases you may need to say** (4 minutes)

Practice these phrases and then test yourself using the cover flap.

أنا حامل.
ena Haamil
I am pregnant.

I have diabetes.	عندي السكر. *Aandee is-sukkar*
I have epilepsy.	عندي صرع. *Aandee sa-raA*
I have asthma.	عندي ربو. *Aandee rabwu*
I have a heart condition.	عندي مشكلة في القلب. *Aandee mushkila fil-elb*
I have a temperature.	عندي حرارة. *Aandee Haraara*
I'm feeling (m/f) faint.	حاسس/ة بالضعف. *Haasis/-a biD-DUAf*
It's urgent.	الحالة مستعجلة. *il-Haala mistaAgila*

5 **Say it** (2 minutes)

My son has diabetes.

I have a pain in my arm.

It's not urgent.

الحالة خطرة؟
il-Haala khaTra
Is it serious?

لا، عندك عسر هضم بس.
laa, Aandik Ausur haDm bass
No, you only have indigestion.

طمنتني!
tamintanee
What a relief!

1 Warm up (1 minute)

Ask "Where are the toilets?" (pp.52-3)

Ask "Is it serious?" (pp.92-3)

What is the Arabic for "mouth" and "head"? (pp.90-1)

Fil-mustashfa
At the hospital

It is useful to know a few basic phrases relating to hospitals and medical treatment for use in an emergency, or in case you have to visit a friend or colleague in hospital. As a visitor you should have adequate insurance to cover any treatment or hospital stay.

2 Useful phrases (5 minutes)

Familiarize yourself with these phrases. Conceal the Arabic with the cover flap and test yourself.

إيه مواعيد الزيارة؟ *eh mawaaʌeed iz-ziyaara*	What are the visiting hours?
حتأخذ وقت قد إيه؟ *нataakhud wa't adda eh*	How long will it take?
حتألم؟ *нat-allim*	Will it hurt?
نام هنا من فضلك. *naam hina, min faɒlak*	Lie down here, please. (to a man)
نامي هنا من فضلك. *naamee hina, min faɒlik*	Lie down here, please. (to a woman)
ما تاكلش حاجة. *maa takulsh нaaga*	Don't eat anything. (to a man)
ما تاكليش حاجة. *maa takleesh нaaga*	Don't eat anything. (to a woman)
افتح فمك من فضلك. *iftaн famak min faɒlak*	Open your mouth, please. (to a man)
افتحي فمك من فضلك. *iftaнee famik min faɒlik*	Open your mouth, please. (to a woman)
لازم نعمل تحليل دم. *laazim naʌmal taнleel dam*	We have to do a blood test.

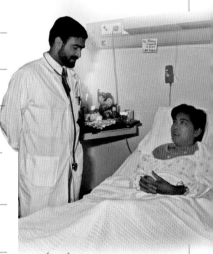

أنت أحسن؟
enti aнsan
Are you feeling better?

فين غرفة الانتظار؟
fayn ghurfit il-intizaar
Where is the waiting room?

Words to remember (4 minutes)

Familiarize yourself with these words and test yourself using the flap.

emergency department	قسم الطوارئ
	qism iт-тawaari'
x-ray department	قسم الأشعة
	qism il-ashiʌa
children's ward	عنبر الأطفال
	ʌanbar il-aтfaal
operating theatre	غرفة العمليات
	ghurfit il-ʌamaliyyaat
waiting room	غرفة الانتظار
	ghurfit il-intizaar
stairs	سلم
	sillim

صورة الأشعة طبيعية.
soorit il-ashiʌa тabeeʌeyya
The x-ray is normal.

---

(4) **Put into practice** (3 minutes)

Join in this conversation. Cover up the text on the right and complete the answering part of the dialog in Arabic. Check your answers and repeat if necessary.

عندك التهاب في الكلى.	الحالة خطرة؟
ʌandak iltihaab fil-kily	il-наala khaтra
You have a kidney infection.	
Ask: Is it serious?	

لازم نعمل تحليل دم.	حتألم؟
laazim naʌmal таhleel dam	наt-allim
We have to do a blood test.	
Ask: Will it hurt?	

---

(5) **Say it** (2 minutes)

Don't move your arm.

Where is the children's ward?

Do I need an x-ray?

Read it The Arabic letter ق is pronounced as a throaty "q" in more formal Arabic, as in the word **qism** (department). But the sound is dropped in informal Egyptian Arabic, turning **qahwa** (coffee) into **ahwa** and **sooq** (market) into **soo'**. In other regions it becomes a hard "g" (**gahwa, soog**). Whichever way it is pronounced, it is always written as ق:

ق (q) + س (s) + م (m) = قسم (qism)

RaagiA wi karrar
Review and repeat

1 The body

❶ رأس
raas

❷ ذراع
diraaA

❸ صدر
sidr

❹ بطن
baтn

❺ رجل
rigl

❻ ركبة
rukba

❼ قدم
qadam

1 The body (4 minutes)

Name the numbered body parts in Arabic.

- ❶ head
- ❷ arm
- ❸ chest
- ❹ stomach
- ❺ leg
- ❻ knee
- ❼ foot

2 On the phone

❶ ممكن أكلم الأستاذ سالم؟
mumkin akallim il-ustaaz saalim

❷ هاري نولز من مطابع كابيتال.
haaree noolz min maтaabiA kabitaal

❸ ممكن أسيب رسالة؟
mumkin aseeb risaala

❹ الاجتماع الساعة تسعة.
il-igtimaaA is-saaAa tisAa

❺ مع السلامة.
maAasalaama

2 On the phone (4 minutes)

You are arranging an appointment. Follow the conversation, replying in Arabic following the English prompts.

aaloh. maAak AZZa barakaat
❶ Can I speak to Mr. Saalim?

meen maAaya?
❷ Harry Knowles from Capital Printers.

il-khatt mashghool
❸ Can I leave a message?

tabAan
❹ The meeting is at 9 o'clock.

maashi. shukran
❺ Goodbye.

3 **Clothing** (3 minutes)

Say the Arabic words for the numbered items of clothing.

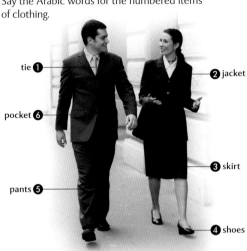

tie **1**

2 jacket

pocket **6**

3 skirt

pants **5**

4 shoes

3 **Clothing**

1 كرافتة
  kravatta
2 جاكتة
  jaketta
3 جيبة
  jeeba
4 جزمة
  gazma
5 بنطلون
  bantalon
6 جيب
  gayb

4 **At the doctor's** (4 minutes)

Say these phrases in Arabic.

1 I don't feel well.

2 I have diabetes.

3 I have a pain in my shoulder.

4 I am pregnant.

4 **At the doctor's**

1 عندي شعور بالتعب.
  ʌandee shuʌoor bit-taʌb
2 عندي السكر.
  ʌandee is-sukkar
3 عندي ألم في كتفي.
  ʌandee alam fi kitfee
4 أنا حامل.
  ena ħaamil

Fil-bayt
At home

1 **Warm up** (1 minute)

Say the months of the year in Arabic. (pp.28–9)

Ask "Where are the toilets?" (pp.52–4)

Say "The lift is out of order." (pp.60–1)

The Arabic word for *house* is **bayt**, and *apartment* is **sha'a**. Many city-dwellers live in *apartment blocks* (**ʌimaaraat**), but more traditional houses can still be found in rural areas. Villas (**villaat**) with gardens are also common in the suburbs of major cities and in tourist resorts.

2 **Match and repeat** (5 minutes)

Match the numbered items to the list and test yourself using the flap.

1 مدخنة
madkhana

2 شباك
shibbaak

3 سطح
saṭн

4 بلكونة
balkohna

5 شيش
sheesh

6 حائط
наa'iт

7 باب
baab

8 جراج
garaaj

1 chimney

2 window

shutters **5**   wall **6**

Cultural tip Most homes in the Arabic-speaking world have shutters at every window and balcony door. These are closed at night and also during the heat of the day in summer to keep the rooms cool. Curtains, where they are used, tend to be for decoration. Many windows also have mesh screens fitted to protect against mosquitos and other insects.

3 Words to remember (4 minutes)

Familiarize yourself with these words and test yourself using the flap.

الإيجار كام في الشهر؟
il-eegaar kaam fish-shahr
How much is the rent per month?

room	غرفة	*ghurfa*
floor	أرضية	*aгвeyya*
ceiling	سقف	*sa'f*
bedroom	غرفة نوم	*ghurfit nohm*
bathroom	حمام	*наmmaam*
kitchen	مطبخ	*meтbakh*
dining room	غرفة سفرة	*ghurfit sufra*
living room	غرفة جلوس	*ghurfit guloos*

3 roof   **4** balcony

7 door   **8** garage

4 Useful phrases (3 minutes)

Practice these phrases and test yourself.

فيها تكييف؟
feehaa takeef

Is there air-conditioning?

فاضية دلوقتي؟
faвya dilwa'ti

Is it vacant now?

الفيلا مفروشة؟
il-filla mafroosha

Is the villa furnished?

5 Say it (2 minutes)

Is there a dining room?

Is the apartment furnished?

Is it vacant in July?

1 Warm up (1 minute)

What is the Arabic for "kitchen," "floor," and "shutters"? (pp.98-9)

Say "beautiful," "old," and "big." (pp.64-5)

Daakhil il-bayt
Inside the house

Villas or apartments can be rented furnished or unfurnished. You will need to check in advance whether the cost of utilities is included in the rent. You may also need to pay a share of the communal upkeep and sometimes contribute to the cost of employing a *bawwaab* (doorman).

2 Match and repeat (3 minutes)

Match the numbered items to the list in the panel below.

❶ كرسي
kursee

❷ حوض مطبخ
ноно meтbakh

❸ ميكرويف
meekroweef

❹ فرن
furn

❺ بوتاجاز
butagaaz

❻ ثلاجة
tallaaga

❼ مائدة
maa'ida

❶ chair

fridge ❻

❹ oven   ❺ range   table ❼

3 In conversation (3 minutes)

الفرن هنا.
il-furn hina
The oven is here.

فيه غسالة كمان؟
feeh ghasaala kamaan
Is there a washing machine as well?

أيوه، وهنا فريزر كبير.
aywah, wi-hina freezar kibeer
Yes, and here is a big freezer.

4 Words to remember (2 minutes)

Familiarize yourself with these words and test yourself using the flap.

الكنبة جديدة.
il-kanaba gideeda
The sofa is new.

closet	دولاب
	doolaab
sofa	كنبة
	kanaba
rug	سجادة
	siggaada
bath	بانيو
	banyo
toilet	تواليت
	twaalett
bathroom sink	حوض حمام
	HoHD Hammaam

② kitchen sink   **③** microwave

5 Useful phrases (4 minutes)

Practice these phrases and then test yourself using the cover flap.

The range isn't working.	البوتاجاز مش شغال.
	il-butagaaz mish shagh-ghaal
Is electricity included?	ده شامل الكهرباء؟
	dah shaamil ik-kahrabaa
The rug isn't clean.	السجادة مش نظيفة.
	is-siggaada mish niDeefa

6 Say it (2 minutes)

Is there a microwave?

The sofa isn't clean.

The oven isn't working.

كل حاجة جديدة جدا.
kullaHaaga gideeda giddan
Everything is very new.

وغسالة الأطباق هنا.
wi-ghasaalit il-aTbaa' hina
And here is the dishwasher.

الحوض جميل!
il-HoHD gameel
The sink is beautiful!

Il-ginayna
The garden

1 **Warm up** (1 minute)

Say "I need." (pp.64–5)

What is the Arabic for "day" and "today"? (pp.28–9)

Say the days of the week. (pp.28–9)

The garden of a house or villa may be communal or partly shared. A charge for the upkeep of the garden may be included in the rent. It is wise to check with the agent. In the Middle East, gardens are usually watered in the late afternoon or evening, after the hottest part of the day has passed.

2 Words to remember (3 minutes)

Familiarize yourself with these words and test yourself using the flap.

ماكينة قص الحشيش *makanit uss il-Hasheesh*	lawn mower
شوكة *shohka*	pitchfork
جاروف *gaaroof*	spade
رشاش *rash-shaash*	sprinkler

1 path

2 tree

3 plants

8 rocks

7 pond

6 palm

3 Useful phrases (4 minutes)

Practice these phrases and then test yourself using the cover flap.

The gardener comes on Sunday.

الجنايني بييجي يوم الحد.
il-gunaynee biyeegee yohm il-Had

Can you cut the grass?

ممكن تقص الحشيش؟
mumkin ti'uss il-Hasheesh

Is the garden private?

الجنينة خاصة؟
il-ginayna khaassa

We need to water the garden.

عاوزين نسقي الجنينة.
Aawzeen nis'ee il-ginayna

4 Match and repeat (5 minutes)

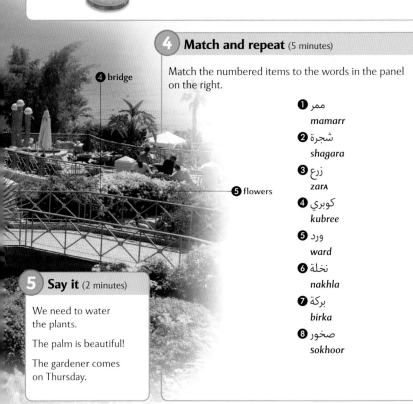

4 bridge

5 flowers

Match the numbered items to the words in the panel on the right.

❶ ممر
mamarr

❷ شجرة
shagara

❸ زرع
zarA

❹ كوبري
kubree

❺ ورد
ward

❻ نخلة
nakhla

❼ بركة
birka

❽ صخور
sokhoor

5 Say it (2 minutes)

We need to water the plants.

The palm is beautiful!

The gardener comes on Thursday.

1 **Warm up** (1 minute)

Say "My name is John."
(pp.8-9)

Say "The pond is
beautiful." (pp.102-03)

What's "fish" in Arabic?
(pp.24-5)

Il-Haywaanaat
Animals

Traditionally, Arabs have valued horses for their speed,
camels for their stamina, and birds of prey for their
grace. Nowadays, house pets such as smaller dogs,
birds, and fish are fairly popular. Cats are usually wild
and live on the streets.

2 **Match and repeat** (3 minutes)

Match the numbered animals to the Arabic words in the
panel on the left. Then test yourself using the cover flap.

❶ عصفور
   Aasfoor

❷ قطة
   otta

❸ سمكة
   samaka

❹ كلب
   kelb

❺ حصان
   Husaan

bird ❶

❷ cat

❸ fish

❺ horse

3 **Useful phrases** (4 minutes)

Learn these phrases and then test yourself using the cover flap.

الكلب ده أليف؟ il-kelb dah aleef	Is this dog friendly?
اسمه إيه؟ ismuh eh	What's his name?
أنا مش غاوي/غاوية قطط. ena mish ghaawee/ ghawya otat	I'm not keen (m/f) on cats.
الكلب ده ما بيعضش. il-kelb dah mabyAoDDish	This dog doesn't bite.

الجمل ده يعض؟
il-gamal dah byAoDD
Does this camel bite?

Cultural tip Large dogs are often kept outside as guard dogs rather than treated as pets. Look out for this sign (*Beware of the dog*). You may also encounter packs of dogs roaming the streets. Give them a wide berth and they will generally avoid you.

احترس من الكلاب

---

4 **Words to remember** (4 minutes)

Familiarize yourself with these words and test yourself using the flap.

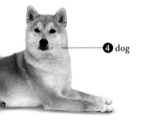
السمكة دي نوعها أيه؟
is-samaka dee nowAha eh
What type of fish is that?

water buffalo	جاموسة	*gamoosa*
sheep	خروف	*kharoof*
cow	بقرة	*ba'ara*
donkey	حمار	*Humaar*
rabbit	أرنب	*arnab*

4 dog

Read it

The in Arabic is **il**. It is written الـ in Arabic script and is always joined to the following word – for example, كلب (**kelb**/dog), الكلب (**il-kelb**/the dog). The **l** sound of **il** sometimes changes to the first letter of the following word, but the script is not affected: السمكة (**is-samaka**/the fish).

---

5 **Put into practice** (3 minutes)

Join in this conversation. Read the Arabic on the left and follow the instructions to make your reply. Then test yourself by concealing the answers with the cover flap.

أيوه، اسمه لاكي. ده كلبك؟
dah kelbik   *aywah, ismuh laakee*
Is this your dog?
Say: Yes, his name is Lucky.

ما بيعضش. أنا مش غاوي كلاب.
ena mish ghaawee kilaab   *mabyAoDDish*
I'm not keen on dogs.
Say: He doesn't bite.

RaagiA wi karrar
Review and repeat

1 Colours

① أبيض
abyaD

② أزرق
azra'

③ حمراء
Hamra

④ أصفر
asfar

⑤ سوداء
sohda

1 Colors (4 minutes)

Complete the sentences with the Arabic word for the color in brackets. Watch out for the masculine and feminine forms.

① il-amees _____ . (white)

② il-banтalon _____ . (blue)

③ il-kravatta _____ . (red)

④ il-ward _____ . (yellow)

⑤ il-gazma _____ . (black)

2 Kitchen

① بوتاجاز
butagaaz

② ثلاجة
tallaaga

③ حوض مطبخ
HOHD meтbakh

④ ميكرويف
meekroweef

⑤ فرن
furn

⑥ كرسي
kursee

⑦ مائدة
maa'ida

2 Kitchen (4 minutes)

Say the Arabic words for the numbered items.

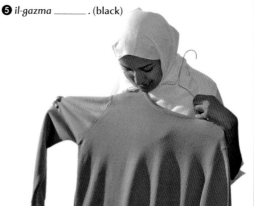

range ①　　　　　fridge ②

chair ⑥

table ⑦

⑤ oven

3 House (4 minutes)

You are visiting a house. Join in the conversation, asking questions in Arabic following the English prompts.

ghurfit il-guloos hina
❶ The rug is beautiful!

aywah, wi-adeema giddan
❷ Is there a dining room as well?

laa, bass feeh maa'ida kibeera fil-metbakh
❸ Is there a garage?

aywah, wi feeh ginayna kamaan
❹ Is it vacant now?

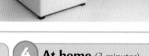

3 House

❶ السجادة جميلة!
is-siggaada gameela

❷ فيه غرفة سفرة كمان؟
feeh ghurfit sufra kamaan

❸ فيه جراج؟
feeh garaaj

❹ فاضية دلوقتي؟
faɒya dilwa'ti

❹ microwave
❸ kitchen sink

4 At home (3 minutes)

Say the Arabic for the following items.

❶ washing machine
❷ sofa
❸ pond
❹ kitchen
❺ tree
❻ garden

4 At home

❶ غسالة
ghassaala

❷ كنبة
kanaba

❸ بركة
birka

❹ مطبخ
metbakh

❺ شجرة
shagara

❻ جنينة
ginayna

Mektab il-bareed wil-bank
Post office and bank

1 Warm up (1 minute)

Ask "How do I get to the station?" and "Where's the post office?"
(pp.50-1, pp.68-9)

What's the Arabic for "passport"? (pp.54-5)

Ask "What time is it?"
(pp.30-1)

The postal service in the Arabic-speaking world is variable and may be slow. If you need to change money, remember that a bank or an exchange bureau will almost always give you a better rate than the foreign exchange desk of a hotel.

2 Words to remember: post (3 minutes)

Familiarize yourself with these words and test yourself using the cover flap to conceal the Arabic on the left.

جواب *gawaab*	letter
طرد *Tard*	parcel
بريد جوي *bareed gawwee*	air mail
طوابع *tawaabiʌ*	stamps
صندوق بريد *sundoo' bareed*	mail box
ساعي البريد *saaʌee l-bareed*	mailman

كارت بوستال
kart bostaal
postcard

ظرف
zarf
envelope

3 In conversation (3 minutes)

عاوز أصرف فلوس.
ʌawiz asrif fuloos

I'd like to change some money.

معاك اثبات شخصية؟
maʌak ithbaat shakhseyya

Do you have identification?

أيوه، معايا جواز السفر.
aywah, maʌaya gawaaz is-safar

Yes, I have my passport.

4 **Words to remember: bank** (2 minutes)

Familiarize yourself with these words and test yourself using the cover flap to conceal the Arabic on the right.

كارت الائتمان
kart il-i'timaan
credit card

فيه ماكينة صرف آلي؟
feeh makeenit sarf aalee
Is there an ATM?

money	فلوس	*fuloos*
ATM/cashpoint	صرف آلي	*sarf aalee*
cashier	صراف	*sarraaf*
notes	بنكنوت	*banknote*
change	فكة	*fakka*
exchange rate	سعر الصرف	*siAr is-sarf*

5 **Useful phrases** (4 minutes)

Learn these phrases and then test yourself using the cover flap.

I'd like to change some money.	عاوز أصرف فلوس. *Aawiz asrif fuloos*
What is the exchange rate?	سعر الصرف إيه؟ *siAr is-sarf eh*
I'd like to send this by air mail.	عاوز أبعث ده بالبريد الجوي. *Aawiz abAat dah bil-bareed il-gawwee*

6 **Say it** (2 minutes)

I'd like to change some dollars.

Do you sell stamps?

Where's the mail box?

وقع هنا من فضلك.
waqqaA hina min faDlak
Sign here please.

عاوز ميات ولا خمسينات؟
Aawiz miyaat walla khamseenaat

Would you like hundreds or fifties?

ميات من فضلك.
miyaat min faDlik
Hundreds, please.

Il-khidmaat
Services

You can combine the Arabic words on these pages with the vocabulary you learned in week 10 to help you explain basic problems and cope with arranging most repairs. When organizing building work or a repair, it's a good idea to agree the price in advance.

1 Warm up (1 minute)

What is the Arabic for "doesn't work"?
(pp.60-1)

What's the Arabic for "today" and "tomorrow"?
(pp.28-9)

2 Words to remember (4 minutes)

Familiarize yourself with these words and test yourself using the flap.

سباك *sabbaak*	plumber
كهربائي *kahrabaa'ee*	electrician
ميكانيكي *mikaneekee*	mechanic
بناء *bannaa*	builder
عامل نظافة *Aaamil naDDaafa*	cleaner
نقاش *na'aash*	decorator
نجار *naggaar*	carpenter

أنا محتاج ميكانيكي.
ena mihtaag mikaneekee
I need a mechanic.

3 In conversation (3 minutes)

غسالة الأطباق مش شغالة.
ghassaalit il-aтbaa' mish shagh-ghaala

The dishwasher doesn't work.

أيوه، الخرطوم بايظ.
aywah il-kharтoom baayiz
Yes, the hose is broken.

ممكن تصلحه؟
mumkin tisallaнoo
Can you repair it?

4 Useful phrases (3 minutes)

Practice these phrases and then test yourself using the cover flap.

Can you clean the bathroom?	ممكن تنظف الحمام؟ mumkin tinaDDaf il-Hammaam
Can you repair the boiler?	ممكن تصلح السخان؟ mumkin tisallaH is-sakh-khaan
Do you know a good electrician?	تعرف كهربائي كويس؟ taAraf kahrabaa'ee kwayyis

ممكن تصلح المكوى؟
mumkin tisallaH il-makwa
Can you repair the iron?

5 Put into practice (4 minutes)

Practice these phrases. Cover up the text on the right and complete the dialog in Arabic. Check your answers and repeat if necessary.

رسومات هندسية
rusoomaat handaseyya
architect's drawings

حابتدي شغل بكرة.
Habtidi shughl bukra
I'll start work tomorrow.

الكرسي بايظ.
il-kursee baayiz
The chair is broken.
Ask: Can you repair it?

ممكن تصلحه؟
mumkin tisallaHoo

لا، محتاج نجار.
laa. miHtaag naggaar
No, you need a carpenter.
Ask: Do you know a good carpenter?

تعرف نجار كويس؟
taAraf naggaar kwayyis

لا، لازم واحد جديد.
laa laazim waaHid gideed
No, you need a new one.

ممكن تجيبه النهاردة؟
mumkin tigeeboo innahaarda
Can you bring it today?

لا، حارجع بكرة الصبح.
laa Hargaa bukra is-subH
No, I'll come back tomorrow morning.

Yeegee
To come

1 Warm up (1 minute)

Say the days of the week in Arabic. (pp.28-9)

How do you say "cleaner"? (pp.110-11)

Say "It's 9.30," "10.45," "12.00." (pp.30-1)

There are several ways of saying *come*. The word *gayy(a)* (coming) can be used with personal pronouns to mean *I'm coming*, *she's coming*, and so on. You need to add the ending *-een* for the plural (*gayyeen*). However, questions using **Aawiz(a)** or **mumkin** require the use of *agee* or *teegee* (see below).

2 To come (6 minutes)

Practice the different ways of saying *come* by reading aloud the phrases below. When you are confident, use the cover flap to conceal the Arabic to test yourself.

أنا/أنت/هو جاي *ena/enta/huwa gayy*	I'm/you're/he's coming (m)
أنا/أنت/هي جاية *ena/enti/heyya gayya*	I'm/you're/she's coming (f)
احنا/أنتم/هما جايين *iнna/entum/ humma gayyeen*	we're/you're/they're coming (pl)
أجي *agee*	I come
تيجي *teegee*	you come (m and f)
ممكن أجي؟ *mumkin agee*	Can I come?
عاوز تيجي؟ *Aawiz teegee*	Do you (m) want to come?
عاوزة تيجي؟ *Aawza teegee*	Do you (f) want to come?

هما جايين بالقطر.
humma gayyeen bil-'aтr
They're coming by train.

Conversational tip
In Arabic the word *gayy(a)* (coming) also means *next* as in *next week* or *next plane*—for example, **mumkin tigee il-usbooa ig-gayy?** (can you come next week?); **it-тayyaara ig-gayya is-saaαa kaam?** (what time is the next plane?).

3 Useful phrases (4 minutes)

Learn these phrases and then test yourself using the cover flap. Notice that there is a special phrase meaning *Come!*

When can I come?	ممكن أجي امتى؟ *mumkin agee imta*
Are you (pl) coming tomorrow?	أنتم جايين بكرة؟ *entum gayyeen bukra*
Do you (m/f) want to come with us?	عاوز(ة) تيجي معانا؟ *Aawiz/-a teegee maAna*
Come! (to a male/ female/group)	تعال (ي/وا) *taAAala/taAAalee/ taAAaloo*

ممكن تيجي يوم الحد؟
mumkin teegee yohm il-Had
Can you come on Sunday?

4 Put into practice (4 minutes)

Practice these phrases. Then cover up the text on the right and say the answering part of the dialog in Arabic. Check your answers and repeat if necessary.

كوافير سوزي. أي خدمة؟
kwafeer suzi. ayyi khidma
Suzi's hair salon.
Can I help you?

Say: I want an appointment, please.

عاوزة ميعاد من فضلك.
Aawza miAaad min faDlik

عاوز تيجي امتى؟
Aawza teegee imta
When do you want to come?

Ask: Can I come today?

ممكن أجي النهاردة؟
mumkin agee innahaarda

أيوه. الساعة كام؟
aywah. is-saaAa kaam
Yes. What time?

Say: I want to come at 10:30.

عاوزة أجي عشرة ونص.
Aawza agee Aashra wi-nuSS

Il-bolees wil-gareema
Police and crime

What's the Arabic for "big" and "small"? (pp.64-5)

Say "The room is big" and "The bed is small." (pp.60-1, pp.64-5)

If you are the victim of a crime while traveling or living overseas, you will need to go to the police station to report it. Initially, you may have to explain your complaint in Arabic, so some basic vocabulary is useful.

2 **Words to remember: crime** (4 minutes)

Familiarize yourself with these words.

سرقة	robbery	
sir'a		
محضر	police report	
maнDar		
حرامي	thief	
нaraamee		
بوليس/شرطة	police	
bolees/shurta		
شاهد	witness	
shaahid		
محام	lawyer	
muнaami		

أنا عاوز محام.
ena лawiz muнaami
I need a lawyer.

3 **Useful phrases** (3 minutes)

Learn these phrases and then test yourself using the cover flap to conceal the Arabic on the left.

أنا اتسرقت.	I've been robbed.
ena itsara't	
سرقوا إيه؟	What was stolen?
sar'oo eh	
شفت الفاعل؟	Did you see who did it?
shuft il-faaлil	
السرقة حصلت امتى؟	When did the
is-sir'a hasalit imta	theft happen?

كاميرا
kameera
camera

محفظة
maнfaza
purse

4 **Words to remember: appearance** (5 minutes)

Learn these words. Remember: adjectives have a feminine form ending in -**a**.

man/woman	رجل/سيدة	raagil/sayyida
tall (m/f)	طويل/طويلة	тaweel/тaweela
short (m/f)	قصير/قصيرة	usayyar/usayyara
young (m/f)	صغير/صغيرة	sughayyar/sughayyara
old (m/f)	عجوز/عجوزة	ʌagooz/ʌagooza
fat (m/f)	سمين/سمينة	sameen/sameena
thin (m/f)	رفيع/رفيعة	rufayyaʌ/rufayyaʌa
his hair/her hair is long	شعره/شعرها طويل	shaʌroo/shaʌraha тaweel
with glasses	بنظارة	bi-naддaara

هو قصير وبشنب.
huwa usayyar wi bi-shanab
He is short, with a mustache.

شعره أسود وقصير.
shaʌroo iswid wi-usayyar
His hair is black and short.

Read it The police are referred to as either *il-bolees* or *ish-shurтa* and this is what you may see written on police cars and stations:

الشرطة   البوليس

---

5 **Put into practice** (2 minutes)

Practice these phrases. Then cover up the text on the right and follow the instructions to make your reply in Arabic.

كان شكله إيه؟   قصير وسمين.
kaan shekloo eh   *usayyar wi-sameen*
What was he like?
Say: Short and fat.

وشعره؟   طويل وأسود.
wi-shaʌroo   *тaweel wi iswid*
And his hair?
Say: Long and black.

RaagiA wi karrar
Review and repeat

il-agweba
Answers Cover with flap

1 To come

❶ جاي
gayy

❷ جايين
gayyeen

❸ أجي
agee

❹ جاية
gayya

❺ تيجي
teegee

1 To come (3 minutes)

Put the correct form of *come* into the gaps.

❶ *enta* _____ *bukra?*

❷ *humma* _____ *bil-qiraar*

❸ *(ena) mumkin* _____ *yohm is-sabt?*

❹ *heyya* _____ *il-usbooA ig-gayy*

❺ *enti Aawza* _____ *maAna?*

2 Bank and post

❶ كارت الائتمان
kart il-i'timaan

❷ كارت بوستال
kart bostaal

❸ طرد
rard

❹ ظرف
zarf

2 Bank and post (4 minutes)

Name these items.

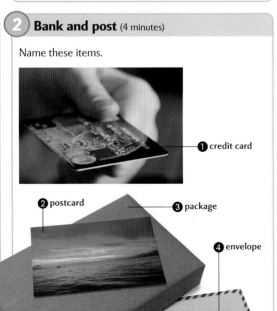

❶ credit card

❷ postcard

❸ package

❹ envelope

3 Appearance (4 minutes)

What do these descriptions mean?

❶ huwa taweel wi-rufayyaʌ

❷ shaʌraha usayyar

❸ ir-raagil usayyar wi bi-naᴅᴅaara

❹ heyya ʌagooza wi-sameena

❺ ena ᴛaweel wi bi-shanab

3 Appearance

❶ He is tall and thin.

❷ Her hair is short.

❸ The man is short (and) with glasses.

❹ She's old and fat.

❺ I am tall with a mustache.

4 The pharmacy (4 minutes)

You are asking a pharmacist for advice. Join in the conversation, replying in Arabic following the English prompts.

ayyi khidma?
❶ I have a cough.

ʌandak bard kamaan?
❷ No, but I have a headache.

ʌandina ʜuboob
❸ Do you have this as a syrup?

aywah. ittafaᴅᴅal
❹ Thank you. How much is that?

4 The pharmacy

❶ عندي كحة.
ʌandee koʜʜa

❷ لا، بس عندي صداع.
laa, bass ʌandee sodaaʌ

❸ عندك ده دواء سائل؟
ʌandak dah dawaa saayil

❹ شكرا. بكام ده؟
shukran. bikaam dah

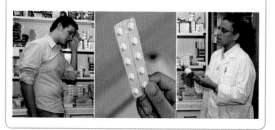

Wa't il-firaagh
Leisure time

1 Warm up (1 minute)

What is the Arabic for "museum" and "library"? (pp.48-9)

Say "I don't like cats." (pp.104-05)

Ask a female "Do you want...?". (pp.22-3)

Like and *prefer* are usually followed by *il* (the): *bitнibb il-fann?* (Do you like art?); *ena bafaддal il-riyaaдa* (I prefer sports). But *il* is usually dropped after the expression *ghaawee/ghaawya* (keen on): *huwa ghaawee masraн* (He is keen on/likes the theater); *heyya ghaawya mooseeqa* (She is keen on/likes music).

2 Words to remember (4 minutes)

Familiarize yourself with these words and test yourself using the cover flap to conceal the Arabic on the left.

مسرح *masraн*	theater
سينما *sinima*	movies
رياضة *riyaaдa*	sport
زيارة المعالم *ziyaarit il-maлaalim*	sightseeing
موسيقى *mooseeqa*	music
فن *fann*	art

أنا بأحب الرقص.
ena buнibb ir-ra's
I like dancing.

3 In conversation (4 minutes)

أهلا! عاوزة تلعبي تنس؟
ahlan! лawza tilлabee tennis
Hello, do you want to play tennis?

أنا مش غاوية رياضة.
ena mish gaawya riyaaдa
I'm not big on sports.

أمال، هواياتك إيه؟
ummaal, hiwayaatik eh
So then, what are your interests?

4 Useful phrases (4 minutes)

Learn these phrases and then test yourself using the cover flap.

بيحب ألعاب الكمبيوتر.
biyнibb alʌaab il-kompyootir
He likes computer games.

What are your (m/f) interests?	هواياتك إيه؟ *hiwayaatak/-ik eh*
I like art.	أنا باحب الفن. *ena buнibb il-fann*
I prefer the movies.	أنا بأفضل السينما. *ena bafaɒɒal is-sinima*
I like (m) the theater.	أنا غاوي مسرح. *ena ghaawee masraн*
I don't like (f) sports.	أنا مش غاوية رياضة. *ena mish ghaawya riyaaɒa*
That's boring.	ده ممل. *dah mumill*

راقصة
raaqisa
dancer

زي تقليدي
ziyy taqleedee
traditional costume

5 Say it (2 minutes)

I like music.

I prefer sport.

I'm not a big fan of computer games.

بأفضل الرقص.
bafaɒɒal ir-ra's
I prefer dancing.

الرقص ممل.
ir-raqs mumill
Dancing is boring.

معلش. أشوفك بكرة.
maʌalesh. ashoofak bukra
Never mind. I'll see you tomorrow.

Ir-riyaaDa wil-hiwaayaat
Sports and hobbies

1 **Warm up** (1 minute)

Ask "Do you (f) want to play tennis?" (pp.118–19)

Say "I like the theater" and "I prefer sightseeing." (pp.118–19)

Say "I'm not big on art." (pp.118–19)

The word **koora** means *ball*, *globe*, or *sphere*. It is placed first in the Arabic names for many sports: **koorat il-qadam** (literally, "ball of the foot"), **koorat is-salla** ("ball of the basket"). *Soccer* is often shortened to simply **il-koora** (*the ball*).

2 Words to remember (5 minutes)

Familiarize yourself with these words and then test yourself.

كرة القدم	soccer	
koorat il-qadam		
كرة السلة	basketball	
koorat is-salla		
السباحة	swimming	
is-sibaaнa		
ركوب الخيل	horse-riding	
rukoob il-khayl		
صيد السمك	fishing	
sayɒ is-samak		
الجري	running	
ig-garee		

باحب الغطس جدا.
buнibb il-ghaтs giddan
I like diving very much.

تنك هواء
tank hawa
oxygen tank

زعانف
zaдaanif
fins

3 Useful phrases (2 minutes)

Learn these phrases and then test yourself.

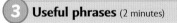

أنا باحب الكرة.	I like soccer.
ena buнibb il-koora	
هي بتحب الجري.	She likes running.
heyya bitнibb ig-garee	
هو بيحب التنس جدا.	He likes tennis very much.
huwa biyнibb it-tennis giddan	

4 biyнibb: to like (4 minutes)

biyнibb is a useful verb meaning *like* or *likes*. The negative is made by putting *ma-* before the verb and *-(i)sh* after it: <u>ma</u>buнib<u>bish</u> (*I don't like*); <u>ma</u>biyнib<u>bish</u> (*he doesn't like*).

I like	(أنا) باحب
	(ena) buнibb
you like (m/f)	(أنت) بتحب/بتحبي
	(enta/enti) bitнibb/-ee
he likes	(هو) بيحب
	(huwa) biyнibb
she likes	(هي) بتحب
	(heyya) bitнibb
What do you like (m) doing?	بتحب تعمل إيه؟
	bitнibb taлmil eh
What do you like (f) doing?	بتحبي تعملي إيه؟
	bitнibbee taлmilee eh
I don't like diving.	ما باحبش الغطس.
	mabuнibbish il-ghaтs
She doesn't like soccer.	ما بتحبش الكرة.
	mabitнibbish il-koora

بتحب/بتحبي المراكب؟
bitнibb/bitнibbee il-maraakib
Do you like (m/f) boats?

نظارة بحر
naддaarit baнr
mask

بدلة غطس
badlit ghaтs
wet suit

5 Put into practice (3 minutes)

Join in this conversation following the English prompts.

أنا باحب التنس.
ena buнibb it-tennis

بتحب تعمل إيه؟
bitнibb taлmil eh
What do you like doing?
Say: I like tennis.

لا، أنا مش غاوي كرة.
laa, ena mish ghaawee koora

بتحب الكرة؟
bitнibb il-koora
Do you like football?
Say: No, I'm not big on football.

أيوه، أنا باحب كرة السلة جدا.
aywah, buнibb koorat is-salla giddan

وكرة السلة؟
wi-koorat-salla
And basketball?
Say: Yes, I like basketball very much.

Iz-ziyaaraat
Socializing

Food and shelter are central to the idea of
hospitality, which is deeply embedded in
Arabic culture. You can expect to receive
numerous invitations from people you
meet, and are likely to be offered generous
amounts of food.

ضيفة
ᴅayfa
guest

2 **Useful phrases** (3 minutes)

Practice these phrases and then test yourself.

عاوزين نعزمكم على العشاء. *ᴧawzeen niᴧzimkum ᴧalal ᴧasha*	We'd like to invite you (pl) to dinner.
يوم الخميس فاضيين؟ *faaᴅiyeen yohm il-khamees*	Are you (pl) free on Thursday?
يوم ثاني، معلش. *yohm taani, maᴧlaysh*	Perhaps another day.

Cultural tip When you visit someone's house for the first
time, it is usual to bring flowers or some cakes. If you are invited
again, having seen your host's house, you can bring something a
little more personal.

3 **In conversation** (6 minutes)

عاوزين نعزمكم يوم الثلاثاء.
ᴧawzeen niᴧzimkum yohm it-talaat

We'd like to invite you
on Tuesday.

آسفة، احنا مشغولين.
aasfa, iнna mash-ghooleen

I'm sorry, we're busy.

طيب والخميس؟
ᴛayyib wil-khamees

OK. What about Thursday?

4 **Words to remember** (2 minutes)

Familiarize yourself with these words and test yourself using the flap.

	party	حفلة
		Hafla
صاحبة البيت	invitation	عزومة
saHbit il-bayt		Aazooma
hostess		

Read it You now know the principles of how Arabic script works and can recognize some individual letters and words. You'll find more information on pp.152–57.

5 **Put into practice** (3 minutes)

Join in this conversation, replying in Arabic.

عاوزين نعزمكم على العشاء بكرة.

Aawzeen niAzimkum Aalal Aasha bukra
We'd like to invite you to dinner tomorrow.

Say: Tomorrow would be very good.

بكرة مناسب جدا.
bukra munaasib giddan

الأكل لذيذ.
il-akl lazeez
The food is delicious.

الساعة ثمانية كويس؟

is-saaAa tamanya kwayyis
Is 8 o'clock OK?

Say: Yes. Thank you for the invitation.

أيوه، شكرا على العزومة.
aywah. shukran Aalal Aazooma

أيوه، الخميس مناسب جدا.
aywah, il-khamees munaasib giddan
Yes, Thursday would be very good.

لازم تيجي مع زوجك.
laazim teegee maAa zohgik
Be sure to bring your husband.

طبعا، شكرا على العزومة.
Tabaan. shukran Aalal Aazooma
Of course. Thank you for the invitation.

RaagiA wi karrar
Review and repeat

1 Animals

1 سمكة
samaka

2 عصفور
Aasfoor

3 أرنب
arnab

4 قطة
oTTa

5 حصان
Husaan

6 كلب
kelb

1 Animals (3 minutes)

Name the numbered animals in Arabic.

1 fish

horse **5**

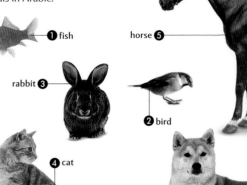

rabbit **3**

2 bird

4 cat

2 Preferences

1 هي مش غاوية غطس.
heyya mish ghaawya ghaTs

2 أنا بأفضل التنس.
ena bafaDDal it-tennis

3 أنا غاوي/غاوية كورة.
ena ghaawee/ ghaawya koora

4 هو مش غاوي ورد.
huwa mish ghaawee ward

2 Preferences (4 minutes)

Say the following in Arabic:

1 She's not big on diving.

2 I prefer tennis.

3 I like soccer.

4 He's not interested in flowers.

3 To like (4 minutes)

Use the different forms of the verb *biyнibb* in these sentences.

❶ ena _____ il-koora

❷ huwa _____ is-sibaaнa

❸ heyya _____ kura is-salla

❹ enti _____ it-tennis?

❺ enta _____ il-ghaтs?

3 To like

❶ بأحب
buнibb

❷ بيحب
biyнibb

❸ بتحب
bitнibb

❹ بتحبي
bitнibbee

❺ بتحب
bitнibb

❻ dog

4 An invitation (4 minutes)

You are invited to dinner. Join in the conversation, replying in Arabic following the English prompts.

faaдiyeen yohm il-khamees?
❶ I'm sorry, we're busy.

тayyib. wis-sabt?
❷ Saturday would be very good.

laazim teegee maдa zohgik
❸ Of course. What time shall we come?

4 An invitation

❶ آسفة، احنا مشغولين.
aasfa, iннa mash-ghooleen

❷ السبت مناسب جدا.
is-sabt munaasib giddan

❸ طبعا. نيجي الساعة كام؟
tabдan. neegee is-saдaa kaam

Reinforce and progress

Regular practice is the key to maintaining and advancing your language skills. In this section you will find a variety of suggestions for reinforcing and extending your knowledge of Arabic. Many involve returning to exercises in the book and using the dictionary to extend their scope. Try going back through the lessons in a different order and mix and match activities to make up your own 15-minute daily program, or focus on topics that are of particular relevance to your current needs.

1 Warm up (1 minute)

Say "I'm sorry." (pp.32-3)

What is the Arabic for "I have an appointment."? (pp.32-3)

How do you say "when?" in Arabic? (pp.32-3)

2 Family (4 minutes)

Say the Arabic for each of the numbered family members. Check you have remembered the Arabic correctly.

father ❶   mother ❷   ❸ daughter   ❺ grandmother
son ❻

Keep warmed up
Re-visit the Warm up boxes to remind yourself of key words and phrases. Work your way through all of them on a regular basis.

Review and repeat again
Work through a Review and repeat lesson as a way of reinforcing words and phrases presented in the course. Return to the main lesson for any topic on which you are no longer confident.

3 In conversation: taxi (2 minutes)

خان الخليلي من فضلك.
Khan il-khalilee min faDlak
Khan il-khalili, please.

Carry on conversing
Re-read the In conversation panels. Say both parts of the conversation, paying attention to the pronunciation.

ماشي. اتفضل.
maashi. ittafaDDal
OK. Please get in.

ممكن أنزل هنا من فضلك؟
mumkin anzil hina min faDlak
Can I get out here, please?

4 Useful phrases (3 minutes)

Learn these phrases and then test yourself using the cover flap.

What time do you open/close?	بتفتحوا/بتقفلوا الساعة كام؟ *bi-tiftaHoo/bi-ti'filoo is-saaAa kaam*
Where are the restrooms?	فين الحمامات؟ *fayn il-Hammaamaat*
Are there facilities for the disabled?	فيه تسهيلات للمعاقين؟ *feeh tas-heelaat lil-muAaqeen*

Practice phrases
Return to the Useful phrases and Put into practice exercises. Test yourself using the cover flap. When you are confident, adapt the phrases, using new words from the dictionary.

Match, repeat, and extend
Remind yourself of words related to specific topics by returning to the Match and repeat and Words to remember exercises. Test yourself using the cover flap. Discover new words in that area by referring to the dictionary and menu guide.

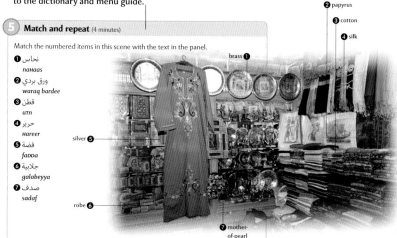

5 Match and repeat (4 minutes)

Match the numbered items in this scene with the text in the panel.

❶ نحاس
naHaas

❷ ورق بردي
waraq bardee

❸ قطن
uTn

❹ حرير
Hareer

❺ فضة
faDDa

❻ جلابية
galabeyya

❼ صدف
sadaf

❶ brass
❷ papyrus
❸ cotton
❹ silk
❺ silver
❻ robe
❼ mother-of-pearl

6 Say it (2 minutes)

Say it again
The Say it exercises are a useful instant reminder for each lesson. Practice these, using your own choice of vocabulary from the dictionary or elsewhere in the lesson.

We need to water the plants.

The palm is beautiful!

The gardener comes on Thursday.

Using other resources

As well as working with this book, try the following ideas to extend and improve your Arabic:

Visit Egypt, or another Arabic-speaking country, and try out your new skills with native speakers. Although this course focuses on Egyptian Arabic, you'll find this is widely understood by Arabic speakers from many regions.

Find out if there is an Arabic community near you. There may be shops, cafés, restaurants, or clubs. Try to visit some of these and use your Arabic to order food and drink and strike up conversations. Most native speakers will be happy to speak Arabic to you.

Join a language class or club. There are often evening and day classes available at a variety of different levels. Or you could start a club yourself if you have friends who are also interested in keeping up their Arabic.

Expand your new knowledge of the Arabic script. Look at the back of food packages and other products. You will often find a list of ingredients or components in Arabic. See if you can spot familiar letters and words and work out some other words by comparing them to the English equivalent.

Find language-learning websites, some of which offer online help and activities.

MENU GUIDE

This guide lists the most common terms you are likely to come across on Arabic menus. The dishes are divided into categories, and the Arabic script is given to help you identify items on a menu.

Appetizers, soups, and salads

سلطة باذنجان	*salaтit baadingaan*	eggplant salad
شوربة فراخ	*shorbit firaakh*	chicken soup
تبولة	*tabboola*	cracked wheat salad
شوربة سمك	*shorbit samak*	fish soup
عصير فواكه	*ʌaseer fawaakih*	fruit juice
سلطة خضراء	*salaта khaдra*	green salad
حمص	*hummus*	hummus—puréed chickpeas
شوربة عدس	*shorbit ʌads*	lentil soup
بطارخ	*baтaarikh*	mullet roe
زيتون	*zaytoon*	olives
سلطة بلدي	*salaта baladee*	Oriental mixed salad
مخلل	*mekhallil*	pickles
سلطة بطاطس	*salaтit baтaaтis*	potato salad
جرجير	*gargeer*	arugula
سلطة	*salaта*	salad
سردين	*sardeen*	sardines
شوربة	*shorba*	soup

ورق عنب	wara' ʌenab	stuffed vine leaves
طحينة	тaнeena	tahini—sesame seed paste
بابا غنوج	baaba ghannoog	tahini with eggplant
سلطة طماطم	salaatit тaмaaтem	tomato salad
شوربة خضار	shorbit khuɒaar	vegetable soup
سلطة زبادي	salaatit zibaadee	yogurt salad

Eggs, cheese, and pasta

بيض مسلوق	bayɒ masloo'	boiled eggs
جبن/جبنة	gibn/gibna	cheese
لبنة	labna	strained yogurt
بيض	bayɒ	eggs
مش	mish	salty cheese
بيض مقلي	bayɒ ma'lee	fried eggs
جبنة رومي	gibna roomee	hard cheese
مكرونة	makarona	macaroni
جبنة قديمة	gibna adeema	mature cheese
شعرية	sheʌreeya	noodles (angel hair)
أومليت	omlayt	omelet
عجة	ʌegga	omelet with onions and parsley
شكشوكة	shakshooka	scrambled eggs with mince
جبنة فلاحي	gibna fallaahee	soft farmer's cheese
مكرونة اسباجيتي	makarona spaghetti	spaghetti
جبنة بيضاء	gibna bayɒa	white cheese

Fish

أنشوجة	*anshooga*	anchovies
كابوريا	*kaaboriya*	crab
تعبان البحر	*tiʌbaan il-bahr*	eel
سمك	*samak*	fish
سمك صيادية	*samak sayyadeeya*	fish with rice
سمك مقلي	*samak ma'lee*	fried fish
سمك مشوي	*samak mashwee*	grilled fish
استاكوزا	*estakoza*	lobster
سمك بوري	*samak booree*	mullet
اخطبوط	*akhtaboot*	octopus
جمبري	*gambaree*	shrimps
سردين	*sardeen*	sardines
قاروص	*aroos*	sea bass
سمك موسى	*samak moosa*	sole
سبيط	*subbayt*	squid
تونة	*toona*	tuna

Meat and fowl

لحم بقري	*lahm ba'aree*	beef
فراخ / دجاج	*firaakh/dajaaj*	chicken
كستليتة / ريش	*kosteleeta/reyash*	cutlets
بط	*batt*	duck
اسكالوب	*eskaalob*	cutlet
فيليتو	*feeletto*	fillet

كباب	kebaab	grilled cubes of meat (usually lamb) on a skewer
لحم ضاني	laнm daanee	lamb
كبدة	kebda	liver
لحم	laнm	meat
كفتة	kofta	meatballs or minced meat on a skewer
لحم مفروم	laнm mafroom	minced meat
مشويات مشكلة	mashweeyaat meshekkila	mixed grill
حمام	hamaam	pigeon
روزبيف	roosbeef	roast beef
شاورمة	shaawerma	sliced spit-roast lamb/ chicken
ديك رومي	deek roomee	turkey
سجق	sogo'	sausages
بتلو	betello	veal

Traditional Arabic dishes

مسقعة	mesa'aлa	eggplant with minced meat
فول بالزيت	fool biz-zayt	fava beans with oil
محشي	maн-shee	stuffed vegetables
كسكس بالضاني	kuskus bid-daanee	couscous—lamb and steamed semolina
فتة	fatta	rice with bread and meat
كباب سمك	kebaab samak	grilled fish on a skewer

فلافل/طعمية	*falaafel/taamayya*	falafel—fried balls of ground beans or chickpeas
كشري	*kosharee*	mixed rice, lentils, pasta, and onions with a piquant sauce
بسلة باللحمة	*bisilla bil-лaнma*	meat cooked with peas
تورلي	*torli*	mixed vegetable stew
طاجن بامية	*тaagin bamya*	okra stew
صفيحة	*sefeeнa*	pastry base topped with minced lamb
ملوخية بالفراخ	*molookheeya bil-firaakh*	traditional soup of greens with chicken

Vegetables

خرشوف	*kharshoof*	artichokes
باذنجان	*baadingaan*	eggplant
بنجر	*bangar*	beetroot
كرمب	*koronb*	cabbage
جزر	*gazar*	carrots
أرنبيط	*arnabeeт*	cauliflower
كرفس	*karafs*	celery
كوسة	*koosa*	zucchini
خيار	*khiyaar*	cucumber
ثوم	*thoom*	garlic
فاصوليا	*fasoliya*	haricot beans
عدس	*лads*	lentils
خس	*khass*	lettuce

بامية	*baamya*	okra
بصل	*basal*	onions
بسلة	*bisilla*	peas
بطاطس	*baтaaтis*	potatoes
فجل	*figl*	radishes
رز	*rozz*	rice
سبانخ	*sabaanekh*	spinach
بصل أخضر	*basal akhвar*	scallions
ذرة	*dorra*	sweetcorn
بطاطا	*baтaaтaa*	sweet potatoes
طماطم	*тamaaтem*	tomatoes
لفت	*lift*	turnips

Fruit and nuts

لوز	*lohz*	almonds
تفاح	*tuffaaн*	apples
مشمش	*mishmish*	apricots
موز	*mohz*	bananas
توت	*toot*	berries
جوز هند	*gohz hind*	coconut
تين	*teen*	figs
جريب فروت	*grayb froot*	grapefruit
عنب	*ʌenab*	grapes
بندق	*bundo'*	hazelnuts
ليمون	*laymoon*	limes/lemons
منجة	*manga*	mangoes

شمام	*shammaam*	melon
برتقال	*borto'aan*	oranges
خوخ	*khohkh*	peaches
فول سوداني	*fool soodaanee*	peanuts
كمثرى	*kommetra*	pears
أناناس	*anaanaas*	pineapple
فزدق	*fuzdu'*	pistachio nuts
برقوق	*bar'oo'*	plums
زبيب	*zibeeb*	raisins
فراولة	*farawla*	strawberries
يوستفندي	*yoostefendee*	tangerines
بطيخ	*baттeekh*	watermelon

Desserts

كريم كرامل	*krem karamel*	crème caramel
حلويات	*нalawiyaat*	dessert
خشاف	*khoshaaf*	dish of stewed fruits
بقلاوة	*ba'laawa*	fine layered pastry and nuts in syrup
سلطة فواكه	*salaтit fawaakih*	fruit salad
عسل	*Aasal*	honey
آيس كريم	*ays kreem*	ice cream
أم علي	*omm Aalee*	"Mother of Ali"— pudding with raisins and milk
كنافة	*kunaafa*	angel-hair pastry with nuts and syrup

رز بلبن	*ruzz bi-laban*	rice pudding
بسبوسة	*basboosa*	semolina cake with syrup
معمول	*maʌmool*	cake stuffed with dates
قشطة	*ishta*	thick cream
ملبن	*malban*	Turkish delight

Drinks

قهوة مضبوط	*ahwa mazboot*	Arabic coffee, medium sweet
قهوة زيادة	*ahwa ziyaada*	Arabic coffee, very sweet
بيرة	*beera*	beer
قهوة	*ahwa*	coffee
قهوة بالحليب	*ahwa bil-haleeb*	coffee with milk
قهوة سادة	*ahwa saada*	coffee without sugar
كولا	*cola*	cola
كركديه	*karkaday*	fuchsia tea
عصير جوافة	*ʌaseer gawaafa*	guava juice
عصير ليمون	*ʌaseer laymoon*	lemon juice
عصير منجة	*ʌaseer manga*	mango juice
مياه معدنية	*mayya maʌdaneyya*	mineral water
شاي بالنعناع	*shaay bin-naʌnaʌ*	mint tea
عصير برتقال	*ʌaseer bortogaal*	orange juice
نبيذ أحمر	*nabeet aнmar*	red wine
صودا	*sooda*	soda water
عصير فراولة	*ʌaseer farawla*	strawberry juice

عصير قصب	Aaseer asab	sugar-cane juice
تمر هندي	tamru hindi	tamarind drink
شاي	shaay	tea
شاي بحليب	shaay bi-Haleeb	tea with milk
مياه	mayya	water
نبيذ أبيض	nabeet abyaD	white wine
نبيذ	nabeet	wine

Basic foods

زبدة	zibda	butter
دقيق	di'ee'	flour
بن	bunn	ground coffee
بهارات	buhaaraat	herbs
مربى	murabba	jelly
حليب/لبن	Haleeb/leban	milk
مستردة	mostarda	mustard
زيت	zayt	oil
فلفل أسود	felfel iswid	pepper (black)
ملح	malH	salt
سكر	sukkar	sugar
شاي	shaay	tea
خل	khall	vinegar
زبادي	zabaadee	yogurt

Types of bread

خبز/عيش	khobz/ʌaysh	bread
بقسماط	bo'somaaт	breadsticks
عيش محمص	ʌaysh miнammas	crispbread
عيش بلدي	ʌaysh baladee	thin round brown bread
سندويتش	sandawitch	sandwich
عيش فينو	ʌaysh feenoo	baguette
عيش شامي	ʌaysh shaamee	white pita bread

Methods of preparation

في الفرن	fil-furn	baked
مشوي على الفحم	mashwee ʌalal-faнm	barbecued
مسلوق	masloo'	boiled
محمر	muнammar	deep-fried
مقلي	ma'lee	fried
مشوي	mashwee	broiled
بالصلصة	bis-salsa	in tomato sauce
محشي	maнshee	stuffed

DICTIONARY
English to Arabic

This dictionary contains the vocabulary from *15-Minute Arabic*, together with many other frequently used words. You can find additional terms for food and drink in the Menu Guide (pp.128–37).

Arabic adjectives (adj) vary according to the gender of the word they describe and whether it is singular or plural. In general, you can add *-a* to refer to the feminine singular <u>and</u> the plural of objects. The most common ending for the plural of words that refer to people is *-een*. Verbs are shown in the masculine singular form of the present tense.

A

about (approximately) *Hawaalee*
accelerator *dawaasit il-benzeen*
accepted *ma'bool*
accident *Hadsa*
accommodation *maskan*
accountant *muHaasib*
ache *alam, wagaA*
adaptor (electrical) *tawSeela*
address *Ainwaan*
adhesive bandage *blaaster*
admission charge *rasm id-dukhool*
after *baAd*
afternoon *baAd iD-Duhr*
aftershave *koloniyit baAd ilHilaa'a*
again *marra tanya, taanee*
against *Didd*
air-conditioning *takeef hawa*
air freshener *muATTir hawa*
air hostess *muDeefa gaweyya*
air mail *bareed gawwee*
aircraft *Tayyaara*
airline *khaTT Tayaraan*
airport *maTaar*
alarm clock *menabbih*
alcohol *koHool*
Algeria *il-gazaa'ir*
all *kull, gameeA;*
  all the streets *kull ish-shawaariA*
allergy *Hassaaseyya*
allowed *masmooH*
almost *ta'reeban*
also *kamaan*
always *dayman*

am: I am *ena*
ambulance *isAaaf*
America *amreeka*
American (man) *amreekaanee;*
  (woman) *amreekaaneyya;*
  (adj) *amreekaanee*
Ancient Egypt *masr il-'adeema*
Ancient Egyptians *qodamaa' il-maSreyyeen*
and *wi, wa*
animal *Haywaan*
ankle *kaaHel*
another (different) *taanee;*
  (additional) *iDaafee*
answering machine *ansar*
antique store *maHall anteekaat*
antiseptic *moTahher*
apartment *sha'a*
apartment block *Λ imaara*
aperitif *mosh-hee*
appetite *shaheyya*
apples *tofaaH*
application form *istimaara*
appointment *miAaad*
apricot *mishmish*
April *abreel*
architecture *il-miAmaar*
are: you are (masculine)
  enta; (feminine) *enti;*
  (plural) *entum;* **we are**
  iHna; **they are** *humma*
area (region) *manti'a*
arm *diraaA*
around *Hawl*
arrivals (airport, etc)
  wuSool
arrive *yohsal*
art *fann*
art gallery *metHaf fonoon*

artist *fannaan*
arts (subject of study)
  il-aadaab
ashtray *menfaDit segaayir*
asleep: he's asleep
  huwwa naayim
asthma *rabwu*
at: at the post office *fi mektab il-bareed;* **at night** *bil-layl;*
  at 3 o'clock *is-saAa talaata;*
  at the traffic circle *Aand id-dawaraan*
attractive *gazzaab*
August *aghusTus*
aunt (maternal) *khaala;*
  (paternal) *Amma*
Australia *ostoraalya*
Australian (man) *ostoraalee;*
  (woman) *ostoraaleyya;*
  (adj) *ostoraalee*
Austria *in-nemsa*
automatic *otomaateeki*
away: far away *baAeed;*
  go away! *imshee!*
awful *weHish giddan*
ax *balTa*
axle *il-aks*

B

baby *Tifl, raDeeA*
baby wipes *waraa'il aTfaal*
back (not front) *wara;*
  (body) *Dahr*
backpack *garabandeyya*
bad *weHish, radee'*
bag *kees, shanTa*
Bahrain *il-baHrayn*
bait *TuAm*
bake *yikhbiz*

baker *khabbaaz*

bakery *makhbaz*

balcony *balkohna*

ball *koora*

ballpoint pen *alam gaaf*

banana *mohza, mohz*

band (musicians) *fir'a*

bandage *robaaт*

bank *bank*

barbecued *mashwee ʌlal-faнm*

barber *нallaa'*

basement *badroom*

basin (sink) *нohD*

basket *salla*

basketball *koorat is-salla*

bath *banyo*; to have
a bath *yistaнamma*

bathrobe *rohb нammaam*

bathroom *нammaam*

battery *baттaareyya*

bazaar *bazaar, soo'*

beach *shaaтi'*

beans *fool*

beard *liнya*

beautiful *gameel*

beauty products
muntagaat tagmeel

because *ʌlashaan*

bed *sireer*

bed linen *melaayaat is-sireer*

bedroom *ghurfit nohm*

beef *laнm ba'aree*

beer *beera*

before *abl*

beginner *mubtadi'*

behind *wara, khalf*

beige *bayj*

bell *garas*

belly dance *ra'S baladee*

below *taнt, asfal*

belt *нizaam*

beside *ganb, bi-gaanib*

best *aнsan, afDal*

better *aнsan*

between *bayn*

bicycle *ʌagala, darraaga*

big *kibeer*

bikini *mayoh bekeenee*

bird *ʌaSfoor*

birthday *ʌeed milaad*; happy
birthday! *ʌeed milaad
saʌeed!* birthday present
hadeeyit ʌeed milaad

bite (verb) *yiʌoDD*; (noun)
ʌDDa; (by insect) *ladgha*

bitter *murr*

black *iswid/sohda*

blanket *baттaneyya*

blind (cannot see) *ʌʌma*

blinds *sitaara*

blister *fa'foo'a*

blood *dam*; blood test
taнleel dam

blouse *bilooza*

blow-dryer *sishwaar*

blue (m/f) *azra/zar'a*

boarding card *kart suʌood*

boat *markib*; (rowing) *qaareb*

body *gism*

boil (verb) *yighlee*

boiled *masloo'*

bolt (noun: on door) *terbaas*

bones *ʌaDm*

book (noun) *kitaab*;
(verb) *yiнgiz*

booking office *mektab il-нagz*

bookstore *mektaba*

boot *boot*

border *нudood*

boring *mumill*

born: I was born in ...;
ena mawlood fi ...

bottle *izaaza*

bottle opener *fattaaнit azaayiz*

bottom (of sea, box, etc) *qaʌ*

box *sundoo'*

boy *walad*

boys *awlaad*

bra *sutyaan*

bracelet *eswera, siwaar*

brakes (noun) *faraamil*

branch *farʌ*

brass *naнaas*

bread *ʌaysh, khubz*

breakdown
(car) *ʌarabeyya ʌтlaana*;
(nervous) *inhiyaar ʌaSabee*

breakfast *fiтaar, fuтoor*

breathe *yitnaffis*; I can't
breathe *mish aa'dir atnaffis*

bridge *kubree, jisr*

briefcase *shanта*

British *biriтaanee*

broiled *mashwee*

broken *maksoor, baayiz*;
broken leg *rigl maksoora*

brooch *brosh*

brother *akh*

brown *bunnee*

bruise *kadma*

brush (for sweeping) *meknasa*;
(paint, tooth) *fursha*

bucket *gardal*

budget (noun) *mizaaneyya*

builder *bannaa*

building *mabnaa*

bumper *iksiDaam*

burglar *liSS*

burn (verb) *yiнra'*; (noun) *нar'*

bus *otohbees, baaS, нaafila*

bus station *maнaттit il-otobeeS*

bus stop *mawqaf otobeeS*

business *ʌamaal*

business card *kart shakhSee*

businessman *raagil ʌamaal*

businesswoman *sayyidit ʌamaal*

busy (occupied) *mashghool*;
(street) *zaнma*

but *bass, laakin*

butcher *gazzaar*

butter *zibda*

button *zoraar*

buy *yishtiri*

by: by the window *ganb/
bi-gaanib ish-shibaak*;

C

cabbage *kurunb*

café *ahwa, maqha*

cake *тorta, kayka*

calculator *aala нaasba*

call: what's it called?
ismuh/ismaha eh?

camel *gamal*

camera *kameera*

campsite *muʌskar*

can: can I have ...? *mumkin ...?*

can (tin) *ʌulba*

can opener *fattaaнit ʌulab*

Canada *kanada*

Canadian (man) *kanadee*;
(woman) *kanadeyya*; (adj)
kanadee

cancer *saraтaan*

candle *shamʌa*

canoe *kaanoo*

cap (bottle) *ghaтaa'*;
(hat) *caab*

car *ʌarabeyya, sayyaara*

car seat (for a baby) *kursee aTfaal*

caravan *karafaan*

carburetor *karboraateer*

card *kart*

careful: be careful! *khalli baalak!*

carpenter *naggaar*

carpet *siggaada*

carrot *gazar*

case (suitcase) *shanTa*

cash *kaash, naqdan;* (coins) *fakka;* **to pay cash** *yidfaA kaash, yidfaA naqdan*

castle *alAa*

cat *oTTa*

catacombs *saraadeeb*

cathedral *kaatedraa'eyya*

cauliflower *arnabeeT*

cave *kahf*

CD *seedee*

ceiling *sa'f*

cell phone *mubayil, maHmool, gawwaal*

cemetery *ma'bara*

center *markaz;* **town center** *wusT il-balad*

certainly *HaaDir*

certificate *shahaada*

chair *kursee*

chambermaid *Aamilit il-fundu'*

change (noun: money) *fakka;* (verb: money) *yiSrif;* (verb: trains, clothes) *yighayyar*

charger (for phone, etc) *shaaHin*

cheap *rakheeS*

check *Hisaab, fatoora, sheek*

checkbook *daftar sheekaat*

check-in *it-tasgeel*

check-out *il-mughaadra*

cheers! (health) *fi SaHHitak!*

cheese *gibna, jubn*

chef *sheef, Tabbaakh*

cherry *kereez*

chess *shaTarang*

chessboard *lawHit ish-shaTarang*

chest (anatomical) *Sidr*

chewing gum *lebaan, masteeka*

chicken *firaakh, dajaaj*

child *Tifl*

children *awlaad, aTfaal*

chimney *madkhana*

China *iS-Seen*

Chinese (man) *Seenee;* (woman) *Seeneyya;* (adj) *Seenee*

chocolate *shokolaata;* **box of chocolates** *Ailbit shokolaata*

church *kaneesa*

cigar *sigaar*

cigarette kiosk *koshk sagaayir*

cigarettes *sagaayir*

city *madeena, balad*

city center *wusT il-balad, wusT il-madeena*

class (school) *faSl;* **first class** *daraga oola;* **second class** *daraga tanya*

classical Arabic *il-fuS-Ha*

classical music *mooseeqa, klaaseekeyya*

clean (adj) *niDeef;* (verb) *yinaDDaf*

cleaner (person) *Aaamil naDDaafa*

clear (obvious) *waaDiH;* (water) *Safee;* **is that clear?** *dah waadiH?*

clever *shaaTir*

client *Aameel*

clock *menabbih, saaAa*

close (near) *urrayyib;* (stuffy) *katma;* (verb) *yi'fil*

clothes *malaabis*

club *naadi;* (cards) *sebaatee*

clutch *debriyaaj*

coach (bus) *otohbees, baaS;* (of train) *Arabeyyit il-qiTaar*

coach station *maHaTTit il-otohbees*

coat *balTo*

coat hanger *shamaaAa*

cockroach *SorSaar*

coffee *ahwa*

coffee pot *kanaka*

coin *Aumla*

cold (illness) *bard;* (adj) *bard, baarid*

collar *yaa'a*

collection (stamps, etc) *magmooAa*

color *lohn*

comb (noun) *meshT;* (verb) *yimashshaT*

come *yeegee;* **I come from ...** *ena min ...;* **we came last week** *gayna il-usbooA illi faat;* **come!** (m/f/pl) *taAaala!/taAaalee!/taAaaloo!*

coming (m/f/pl) *gayy/ gayya/gayyeen*

company (business) *sherika*

complicated *muAaqqad*

computer *kombyootir*

computer games *alAaab il-kombyootir*

concert *Hafla mooseeqeyya*

conditioner (hair) *balsam shaAr*

conductor (bus) *komsaree;* (orchestra) *qaa'ed il-orkestra*

conference *mu'tamar*

congratulations! *mabrook!*

constipation *imsaak*

consulate *unSuleyya*

contact lenses *Aadasaat laaSiqa*

contraceptive *maaniA lil-Haml*

contract *Aa'd*

cook (noun) *Tabbaakh;* (verb) *yuTbukh*

cookie *baskaweet*

cool *baarid*

copper *naHaas*

cork *fell*

corkscrew *barreema*

corner *rukn;* (street) *naSya*

corridor *mamarr*

cosmetics *mustaHDaraat tagmeel*

cost (verb) *yitkallif;* **what does it cost?** *bi-kaam dah?*

cotton *uTn*

cotton wool *uTn Tibbee*

cough (verb) *yikoHH, yisAal;* (noun) *koHHa, soAaal*

country (state) *dawla;* **country** (not town) *reef*

course (dish) *Taba';* **main course** *iT-Taba' ir-ra'eesee*

cousin (male) (paternal) *ibn Aamm;* (maternal) *ibn khaal;* (female) (paternal) *bint Aamm;* (maternal) *bint khaal* cow *ba'ara*

crab *kaboria*

cramp *taqallos il-aDalaat*

cream *kreem*

credit card *kart/biTaa'it i'timaan*

crew *Taaqem*

crib *sireer aTfaal*

crime *gareema*

crowded *zaHma*

cruise *riHla baHreyya*

crutches *AOkkaaz*

cry (weep) *yibkee*; (shout) *yiSeeH*

cucumber *khiyaar*

cup *fingaan*

cupboard *doolaab*

curtains *sataayir*

customs *gamaarik*

cut (noun) *aTA*; (verb) *yi'TaA, yi'uSS*

D

dad *baba*

dairy (shop) *labbaan*

dairy products *muntagaat albaan*

damp *reTooba*

dance/dancing *ra'S*

dangerous *khaTar*

dark *Dalma, meDallim*

daughter *bint, ibna*

day *yohm*

dead *mayyit*

deaf *aTrash*

dear (person) *Azeez*; (expensive) *ghaalee*

December *disembir*

deck chair *kursee blaaj*

decorator *naqqaash*

deep *Ameeq*

degree (university) *shihaada*

deliberately *Amdan*

delicious *lazeez*

delivery *tasleem*

dentist *doktoor/Tabeeb asnaan*

dentures *Taqm asnaan*

deny *yinkir*

deodorant *diodoraan*

department *qism*

departure *raHeel*

departures (airport, etc) *mughadra*

desert *SaHraa'*

designer *muSammim*

dessert *il-Hilw*

diabetes (maraD) *is-sukkar*

diamond (jewel) *il-maas*; (cards) *id-deenaaree*

diapers *Hafaadaat*

diarrhea *is-haal*

diary (agenda) *ajenda*; (journal) *mufakkera*

dictionary *qaamoos*

die *yimoot*

diesel *deezil*

different *mukhtalif*;

difficult *saAb*

dining room *ghurfit is-sufra/ iT-TaAaam*

dinner *Aashaa'*

direction *ittigaah*

directory (telephone) *daleel*

dirty *wisikh, qazer*

disabled *muAaqeen, Aagaza*

dishes (menu) *aTbaaq*

dishwasher *ghasaalit il-aTbaa*

disposable diapers *HafaaDaat*

dive *yighTas*

dive boat *markib ghaTs*

diving *ghaTs*

diving board *menaSSit il-ghaTs*

divorced (man) *muTallaq*; (woman) *muTallaqa*

do *yaAmal*

doctor *doktoor, Tabeeb*

document *watheeqa*

dog *kelb*

doll *Aroosa*

dollar *dolaar*

donkey *Humaar*

door *baab*

double room *ghurfa li-shakhSayn*

down *asfal*

drawer *dorg*

dress *fustaan*

drink (verb) *yishrab*; (noun) *mashroob*; would you like a drink? *tishrab(ee) Haaga?*

drive (verb) *yisoo'*

driver *sawwaa', saa'iq*

driver's license *rukhsit qiyaada*

drops *nu'aT*

drunk *sakraan*

dry *gaaf*

dry cleaner *maHall tanDeef*

during *khilaal*

dust cloth *minfaDa*

duty-free *aswaa' Horra*

E

each (every) *kull*

ear *uzun, widn*

early *badree, mubakkir*

earrings *Hala'*

east *sharq*

easy *sahl*

eat *yaakul*

eggs *bayD*

Egypt *musr*

eight *tamanya*

either: either of them *ayy minhum*; either ... or *ya'ima ... aw ...*

elastic band *astik*

elbow *kOOA*

electric *bik-kahrabaa*

electrician *kahrabaa'ee*

electricity *kahrabaa*

elevator *asanseer, miSAad*

else: anything else *Haaga tanya*; someone else *waaHid taanee*; somewhere else *makaan taanee*

email *email*

email address *Aunwaan il-eemail*

embarrassed *maksoof*

embassy *sifaara*

embroidery *taTreez*

emerald *zumorrod*

emergency *Tawaari'*

Emirates *il-imaaraat*

employee *muwazzaf*

empty *faaDee*

end *nihaaya*; (last) *aakhir*

engaged (couple) *makhToobeen*; (occupied) *mashghool*

engine (motor) *motoor, muHarrik*

engineering *handasa*

England *ingeltera*

English *ingleezee*; (language) *ingleezee* (man) *ingleezee* (woman) *ingleezeyya*

enlargement *takbeer*

enough *kifaaya*

entertainment *tasleyya*

entrance *dukhool, madkhal*

entrance tickets *tazaakir id-dukhool*

envelope *Zarf, maZroof*

epilepsy *saraA*

equipment *Aidda*

eraser *asteeka*

escalator *sillim bik-kahrabaa*

especially *makhSooS*

evening *masaa*

every *kull*

everyone *kulliwaaHid*

everything *kulliHaaga*

everywhere *kullimakaan*

example *misaal*; for example *masalan*

excellent *mumtaaz*

excess baggage *wazn zaayed*

exchange (verb) *yibaadil*

exchange rate *siAr iS-Sarf*

excursion *nuzha*

excuse me! (to get attention) *law samaHt!*

exhibition *maAraD*

exit *makhrag*

expensive *ghaalee*

experienced *maahir*

extension *tamdeed*

eye *Ayn*; eyes *Aynayn*

eye drops *nu'aT lil-Ayn*

F

face *wish, wajh*

facilities (equipment, etc) *tas-heelaat*

faint (unclear) *baahit*; I feel faint *Haasis biD-DuAf*

fair (funfair) *malaahee*; (just)

false teeth *Ta'msnaan*

family *usra, Aela*; my family *usritee; Aeltee*

fan (ventilator) *marwaHa*; (enthusiast) *muAgab*

fan belt *sayr il-marwaHa*

far *biAeed*; how far is it? *il-masaafa adda eh?*

fare *ogrit is-safar*

farm *mazraAa*

farmer *muzaariA*

fashion *il-mohDa*

fast *sareeA*; (noun: during Ramadan, etc) *Sohm*

fat (of person) *sameen, badeen*; (on meat) *dihn*

father *ab, waalid*

faucet *Hanafeyya, Sanboor*

February *febraayir*

feel (touch) *yilmis*;

ferry *Aabbaara*

fever *Homma*

fiancé *khaTeeb*

fiancée *khaTeeba*

field (of study) *magaal*; (meadows) *meroog*

fig *teen*

filling (tooth) *Hashoo*

film *film*

filter *filtir*

finger *SobaaA*

fins *zAaanif*

fire *naar*; (blaze) *Haree'a*

fire extinguisher *Taffaayit Haree'*

fireworks *sawareekh*

first *awwal*; first aid *isAaafaat awwaleyya*; first floor *id-door il-awwal*

fish (singular) *samaka*; (plural, food) *samak*

fishing *sayd is-samak*

fishing boat *markib sayd*

fishing rod *sinnaara*

fish seller *sammaak*

five *khamsa*

fizzy *fawwaar*

flag *Aalam*

flash (camera) *flaash*

flashlight *misbaaH yadawee*

flat (level) *musaTTaH*; (apartment) *sha'a*

flavor *TaAm*

flea *burghooth*

flight *riHlit Tayaraan*

flip-flops *shibshib*

floor (of room) *arDeyya*

flour *di'ee'*

flowers *ward, zuhoor*

flu *inflooenza*

fly (verb) *yiTeer*; (insect) *debaana*

fog *Dabaab*

folk music *mooseeqa haAbeyya*

food *akl, TaAaam*; poisoning *tasammum*

foot *qadam*

for *Aalashaan, li*; for me *Aalashaanee*

foreigner *agnabee*

forest *ghaaba*

fork *shohka*

fountain pen *alam Hibr*

four *arbaAa*

fourth *ir-raabiA*

fracture *kasr*

France *faransa*

free (of) *khaali* (min); (no cost) *maggaani*; (available) *faaDi*

freezer *freezir*

French *faransee*

French fries *baTaaTis muHamarra*

Friday (yohm) *il-gumAa*

fridge *tallaaga*

fried *ma'lee*

friend *SaaHib, Sadeeq*

friendly *laTeef*; (tame) *aleef*

front: in front of *udaam, amaam*

frost *saqeeA*

frozen products *muntagaat mugammada*

fruit *fawaakih*

fruit juice *AaSeer fawaakih*

fry *yi'lee*

frying pan *Taasit il-alee*

full *malyaan*; I'm full *ena shabAaan*

full board *iqaama kamla*

funnel (for pouring) *qumA*

funny *muDHik*; (odd) *ghareeb*

furnished *mafroosh*

furniture *athaath*

G

garage *garaaj*

garden *ginayna, Hadeeqa*

gardener *gunaynee*

garlic *toom*

gas *benzeen*

gas station *maHaTTit benzeen*

gate (airport, etc) *bawwaaba*

gear (equipment) *Aidda*

gearbox *Sundoo' it-tiroos*

German *almaanee*

Germany *almaanya*

get (fetch) *yigeeb*; have you got ...? *Andak/-ik ...?*

get back: we get back tomorrow; *nirgaA bukra*

get in *yudkhul*; (arrive) *yohsil*
get off (bus, etc) *yinzil*
get out *yukhrug*
get up (rise) *yi'oom*
gift *hideyya*
girl *bint*
girls *banaat*
give *yeddee, yaATee*
glad *mabsooT*; **I'm glad** *ena mabsooT*
glass (material) *izaaz, zugaag*; (for drinking) *kubayya, koob*
glasses (spectacles) *naDaara*
gloves *gwentee*
glue *Samgh*
go *yirooH*
goggles *naDaarit mayya*
going (m/f/pl) *raayiH/ raayHa/raayeen*
gold *dahab*
good *kwayyis*; **good morning** *sabaaH il-khayr*; **good afternoon/evening** *masaa' il-khayr*
goodbye *maAasalaama*
government *Hukooma*
granddaughter *Hafeeda*
grandfather *gidd*
grandmother *gidda*
grandson *Hafeed*
grapes *ainab*
grass (lawn) *Hasheesh, Aushb*
gray *ramaadee*
great! *Aazeem!*
Great Britain *bireeTaanya il-Auzma*
Greece *il-yoonaan*
Greek *yoonaanee*
green (m/f) *akhDar/khaDra*
grill *shawwaaya*
grocery *ba'aal*
first floor *id-door il-arDee*
guarantee (noun) *Damaan*; (verb) *yiDman*
guard *Haaris*
guest *Dayf*
guidebook *daleel siyaaHi*
guitar *gitaar*
Gulf *il-khaleeg*
Gulf States *duwwal il-khaleeg*
gun (rifle) *bundu'eeya*; (pistol) *musaddas*

H

hair *shaAr*
haircut (for man) *Helaaqit ish-shaAr*; (for woman) *uSS ish-shaAr*
hairdresser *Hallaaq, kwaafeer*
half *nuSS*; **half an hour** *nuSS saaAa* **half past two** *itnayn wi-nuSS*
hammer *shakoosh, miTraqa*
hand *yad, eed*
handbrake *faraamil yad*
handkerchief *mandeel*
handle (door) *mi'baD*
handsome *waseem*
happy *saAeed, mabsooT*
harbor *meena*
hard *naashif, qaasee*; (difficult) *SaAb*
hat *burnayta, qubaAa*
have (own) *yamtalik*; **I have ...** *Aandee ...*; **I don't have ...** *ma Aandeesh ...*; **can I have ...?** *mumkin ...?*; **have you got ...?** *Andak/-ik ...?*; **I have to go now** *laazem amshee dilwa'tee*
hay fever *Homma l-'ash*
he *huwa*
head *raas*
head office *markaz ra'eesee*
headache *sodaaA*
headlights *fanoos (amaamee)*
headphones *sammaaAaat*
hear *yismaA*
hearing aid *samaaAaat il-aSamm*
heart *elb*
heart attack *nawba elbeyya*
heating *tadfe'a*
heavy *ti'eel*
heel *kaAb*
hello *ahlan*; (on the telephone) *aaloh*
help (noun) *musaaAada*; (verb) *yisaaAid*; **help!** *in-nagda!*;
hepatitis *iS-Sufraa*
her: it's her *dee heyya*; **it's for her** *dah Aalashaan-ha*; **her book** *ketaabha*; **her house** *baytha*; (possessive) *-ha* **it's hers** *dah bitaaAha*

here *hina*
hi *salaam*
hieroglyphs *heeroghleefee*
high *Aaalee*
hill *tell*
him: it's him *dah huwa*; **it's for him** *dah Aalashaan-uh*
hire *yia'ggar, yista'gir*
his ...-uh; his book *ketaabuh*; **his house** *baytuh*
history *taareekh*
hitchhiking *otostop*
HIV positive *mareeD HIV*
hobby *hiwaaya*
Holland *holanda*
honest *Saadi', ameen*
honey *Aasal*
honeymoon *shahr il-Aasal*
hood (car) *kabboot*
horn (car) *kalaks*; (animal) *arn*
horrible *fazeeA*
horse *HuSaan*
horse-riding *rukoob il-khayl*
hose *kharToom*
hospital *mustashfa*
host *SaHb il-bayt*
hostess *SaHbit il-bayt*
hot (water) (mayya) *sukhna*; (weather) *Harr*
hotel *fundu'*
hour *saaAa*
house *bayt, manzil*
household products *muntagaat manzileyya*
how? *izzay? kayf?*; **how many?** *kaam?*; **how much?** *bikaam?*
hundred *meyya*
hungry: I'm hungry *ena gaAaan*
**hurry: I'm in a hurry; ena mustaAgil*
husband *zohg*

I

I *ena*
ice *telg*
ice cream *ays kreem*
ice cube *Hittit telg*
identification *ithbaat shakhSeyya*
if *iza, lau*
ignition *ik-kontakt*
ill *mareeD*

immediately *fawran*

important *muHimm*

impossible *mustaHeel*

in *fi*; in English *bil-ingleezee*;

included *shaamil*

India *il-hind*

Indian (man) *hindee*; (woman) *hindeyya*; (adj) *hindee*

indigestion *Ausur haDm*

infection *Adwa, iltihaab*

information *maAloomaat*

inhaler (for asthma, etc) *bakh-khaakha*

injection *Hu'na*

injury *iSaaba*

ink *Hibr*

inner tube *anboob daakhilee*

insect *Hashara*

insect repellent *Taarid lil-Hasharaat*

inside *daakhil*

insomnia *araq*

insurance *ta'meen*

interest (hobby) *hiwaaya*

interesting *shayyiq*

internet *internet*

interpret *yitargim*

invitation *Aozooma, daAwa*

invite *yiAzim*

invoice *fatoora*

Iraq *il-Airaaq*

Ireland *irlanda*

Irish *irlandee*

Irishman *irlandee*

Irishwoman *irlandeyya*

iron (metal) *Hadeed*; (for clothes) *makwa*

ironmonger *Haddaad*

is: he is ... *huwa ...*; she is ... *heyya ...*

Islam *islaam*

island *gazeera*

it *huwa, heyya*

Italy *eeTaalya*

itch (noun) *Hakka gildeeya*

J

jacket *jaketta*

January *yanaayir*

jazz *mooseeqa il-jazz*

jealous *ghayraan*

jeans *jeenz*

jelly *murabba*

jellyfish *qandeel il-baHr*

jeweler *gawaahirgee*

job *waZeefa*

joke *nukta*

Jordan *il-urdunn*

journey *riHla*

juice *AaSeer*

juice bar *maHall AaSeer*

July *yoolyo*

jumper *buloofar*

junction *taqaatuA*

June *yoonyo*

just: he's just gone out *lissa khaarig*; just two *itnayn bass*

K

keen on *ghaawi*

key *moftaaH*

keyboard *keebord*

kidney *kolya*

kilo *keelo*

kilometer *keelometr*

kitchen *meTbakh*

knee *rukba*

knife *sikkeen*

knitting *it-tereeko*

know *yaAraf*; I don't know *ma aArafsh*

Kuwait *il-kuwayt*

L

label *biTaa'a*

lace *dantella*

laces (of shoe) *robaaT il-gazma*

lake *buHayra*

lamb *kharoof Soghayyar*

lamp *lamba, miSbaaH*

lampshade *abajoora*

land (noun) *arD*; (verb) *yuhbuT*

language *lugha*

laptop *kombyootir maHmool*

large *kibeer*

last (final) *akheer*; last week *il-usbooA illi faat*; last month *ish-shahr illi faat*; at last! *akheeran!*

late *mit'akh-khar*; the bus is late *il-otobees mit'akh-khar*

later *baAdayn*

laugh *yiDHak*

laundromat *maghsala*

laundry (place) *maghsala*; (dirty clothes) *il-ghaseel*

law *qanoon*; (subject of study) *il-Huqooq*

lawn mower *makanit uss il-Hasheesh*

lawyer *muHaami*

laxative *mussah-hil*

lazy *kaslaan*

leaf *wara'it shagar*

learn *yitAallim*

leather *gild*

leave *yiSeeb*

Lebanon *libnaan*

lecture *muHaDra*

lecture hall *qaaAit muHaDraat*

left (not right) *shimaal, yasaar*

left luggage (locker) *khizaanit shonaT*

leg *rigl*

leisure time *wa't il-faraagh*

lemon *lamoon*

lemonade *lamoonaata*

length *Tool*

lens *Aadasa*

less *a'all*

lesson *dars*

letter (mail) *gawaab*; (alphabet) *Harf*

letter box *Sundoo' il-bareed*

lettuce *khass*

library *mektaba*

Libya *leebya*

license *rukhSa*

license plate *lawHit il-arqaam*

life *Hayaa*

life jacket *sutrit in-najaah*

lift (could you give me?) *mumkin tiwassalnee?*

light (not heavy) *khafeef*; (not dark) *faatiH*; (illumination) *noor*

lighter *wallaaAa, qadaaHa*

like: I like swimming *ena buHibb is-sibaaHa*; that's like ... *dah zayy ...*; what does he look like? *shekloo eh?*

lime (fruit) *lamoon*

line *khaTT*; the line is busy *il-khaTT mashghool*; (queue) *Saff*;

lip salve *marham shiffa*

lipstick *rooj*

list *qaa'ima, lista*

liter *litr*

little (small) *sughayyar*; **just a little** *shwayya bass*

liver (human) *kabid*

living room *ghurfit guloos*

lobster *estakoza*

local *maHallee*

lollipop *maSSaaSa*

long *Taweel*; **how long does it take?** *yaakhud kaam wa't?*

lost: I'm lost! *ena tuht!*

lost property *mafqoodaat*

lot: a lot *kiteer, kimeeya kibeera*

loud (noise) *Aaalee*; (color) *Sarikh*

lounge *Saala*

love (noun) *Hubb*; (verb) *yiHibb*

lover (man) *Asheeq*; (woman) *Asheeqa*

low *waaTi, munkhafiD*

luck *Hazz*; **good luck!** *Hazz saAeed!*

luggage *shonat, Haqaa'eb*

luggage rack *raff il-Haqaa'eb*

lunch *ghada*

M

magazine *magalla*

mail (noun) *bareed*; (verb) *yursil bil-bareed*

mail box *sundoo' bareed*

mailman *SaaAee l-bareed*

main street *shaareA rayeesee*

make (manufacture) *yaSnaA*

make-up *makyaaj*

man *raagil*

manager *mudeer*

map *khareeTa*; **a map of Riyadh** *khareeTit ir-riyaaD*

marble *rukhaam*

March *maaris*

margarine *marjareen*

market *soo'*

marmalade *murabbit burtu'aan*

married *mitgawwiz*

mascara *maskaara*

Mass (church) *quddaas*

mast *Saaree*

match (light) *kebreet*; (sports) *matsh, mubaara*

material (cloth) *umaash*

matter: what's the matter? (m/f) *maalak?/maalik?*

mattress *martaba*

Mauritania *moretaanya*

May *maayo*

maybe *yimkin*

me: it's me (speaking) *ena batkallim*; **it's for me** *dah Aalashaanee*

meal *wagba*

meat *laHma, laHm*

mechanic *mikaneekee*

medicine *dawa*; (subject of study) *iT-Tibb*

meet (verb) *yi'aabil*

meeting *igtimaaA*

melon *shammaam*

men's restroom *towaalett lir-rigaal*

menu *menu, qaa'ima*

message *risaala*

middle: in the middle *fil-wusT*

midnight *nuSS il-layl*

milk *Haleeb, laban*

mine: it's mine *dah bitaaAee*

mineral water *mayya maAdaneyya*

mint *naAnaaA*

minute *da'ee'a*; **five minutes** *khamas da'aayi'*

mirror *miraaya*

Miss *aanisa*

mistake *ghalTa*; **to make a mistake** *yighlaT*

modem *modem*

monastery *dayr*

Monday (yohm) *il-itnayn*

money *fuloos*

monitor (computer) *shaasha*

month *shahr*

monument *nusob tizkaaree*

moon *amar*

more *aktar*

morning *SabaaH*; **in the morning** *iS-SubH, fiS-Sabaah*

Morocco *il-maghrib*

mosaic *fosayfesaa'*

mosque *masgid, gaamiA*

mosquito *naamoosa, baAooDa*

mother *omm, waalida*

mother-of-pearl *sadaf*

motorbike *motosikl*

motorboat *lansh, qaareb*

motorway *Tareeq Horr*

mountain *gebel*

mouse *faar*

mouth *fum, bo'*

move *yitHarrak*; (house) *yoAzzil*

movie *film*

movies *is-seenima*

movie theater *sinima*

Mr. *il-ustaaz, is-sayyid*

Mrs. *il-ustaaza, is-sayyida*

much: not much *mish kiteer*; **much better** *aHsan kiteer*

mug *fingaan kibeer*

mule *baghl*

mum *mama*

museum *metHaf*

mushroom *fuTr*

music *mooseeqa*

musical instrument *aalaa mooseeqeyya*

musician *mooseeqaar*

Muslim *muslim*

mussels *umm il-khulool*

mustache *shanab*

mustard *mostarda, khardal*

my *...-ee*; **my book** *kitaabee*; **my bag** *shanTitee*; **my keys** *mafaateeHee*

mythology *asaaTeer*

N

nail (metal) *mosmaar*

nails (finger) *dawaafir*

nailfile *mabrad dawaafir*

name *ism*

napkin *foo-Ta*

narrow *Dayya'*

near *urrayyib min, ganb*

necessary *Darooree*

neck *ra'aba*

necklace *Au'd*

need (verb) *yiHtaag*; **I need ...** *ena miHtaag ...*; **there's no need** *mafeesh daaAee*

needle *ibra*

negative *salbee*

nephew (brother's son) *ibn il-akh*; (sister's son) *ibn il-ukht*

never *abadan*

never mind *maAlesh*

new *gideed*
New Zealand *niyoo zilanda*
New Zealander (man) *niyoo zilandee*; (woman) *niyoo zilandeyya*
news *akhbaar*
newspaper *gornaal, gareeda*
newsstand *maHal iS-SuHuf*
next *ig-gaay*; **next week** *il-usbooA ig-gaay*; **next month** *ish-shahr ig-gaay*
next to *ganb*
nice *kwayyis, gameel*
niece (brother's daughter) *bint il-akh*; (sister's daughter) *bint il-ukht*
night *layla*; **three nights** *talat leyaalee*
night porter *mudeer laylee*
nightclub *naadee laylee*
nightgown *amees nawm*
Nile *in-neel*
nine *tisAa*
no (response) *laa*; **I have no ...** *maa Andeesh ...*; **there are no ...** *ma feesh ...*
noisy *dawsha*
noon *iD-Duhr*
north *shamaal*
Northern Ireland *irlanda ish-shamaaleyya*
nose *anf*
not *mish*
notepad *nota*
nothing *walla Haaga*
novel *riwaaya*
November *nofembir*
now *dilwa'ti, alaan*
number *raqm, nimra*
nurse (m/f) *mumarriD/a*
nut (for bolt) *Saamoola*
nuts (dried fruit) *mukassaraat*

O

o'clock: **3 o'clock** *is-saAa talaata*
obelisk *masalla*
occasionally *aHyaanan*
October *oktobir*
octopus *akhTaboot*
of course *TabAan*
office *mektab*

often *kiteer, ghaaliban*
oil (for food, engine) *zayt*; (crude) *betrool*
oil industry *SinaaAit il-betrool*
oil wells *aabaar betrool*
ointment *marham*
OK *maashi, Tayyib, kwayyis*
old (thing) *adeem*; (person) *Aagooz*
olives *zaytoon*
Oman *Aomaan*
omelet *omlayt*
on *Aala*; **on the ground** *Aalal-arD*
one *waaHid*
onion *basal*
only *bass, faqaT*
open (verb) *yiftaH*; (adj) *maftooH*
opening hours *mawaAeed il-Aamal*
opera *obra*
opera house *daar il-obra*
opposite: **opposite the hotel** *udaam il-fundu'*
optician *naDaaraatee*
or *aw*
orange (color) *burtu'aanee*; (fruit) *burtu'aan*
orange juice *AaSeer burtu'aan*
orchestra *orkestra*
ordinary (normal) *Aadee*
organ *AuDw*; (music) *orghon*
our *-na*; **it's ours** *dah bitaaAna*
out: **he's out** *huwa mish mawgood*
out of order *AaTlaan*
outside *barra, khaarig*
oven *furn*
over *foh'*; **over there** *hinaak*
overtake *yit-khaTTa*

P

package *Tard*
packet *Aulba*; **a packet of ...** *Aulbit ...*
padlock *ifl*
page *SafHa*
pain *alam*
paint (noun) *booya*
pair *gohz*
pajamas *bijaama*

Pakistan *baakistaan*
Pakistani (man) *baakistaanee*; (woman) *baakistaaneyya*; (adj) *baakistaanee*
Palestine *filasTeen*
Palestinian (man) *filasTeenee* (woman) *filasTeeneyya*
Palestinian (adj) *filasTeenee*
palm *nakhla*
pants *banTalon*
paper (material) *waraq*
papyrus *waraq bardee*
pardon? *naAm? afandim?*
parents *waalidayn*
park (noun) *gunayna, Hadeeqa*; **where can I park?** *arkin fayn?*
party (celebration) *Hafla*; (group) *magmooAa*; (political) *Hizb*
passenger *raakib*
passport *gawaaz is-safar*
password *kilmit il-muroor*
pasta *makarona*
pastry shop *Halawaanee*
path *mamarr, mamsha*
pay *yidfaA*
payment *dafA*
peach *khohkh*
peanuts *fool soodaanee*
pear *kometra*
pearl *lu'lu'*
peas *bisilla*
pedestrian *mushaa*
peg (clothes) *mashbak ghaseel*
pen *alam*
pencil *alam ruSaaS*
pencil sharpener *barraaya*
penpal *Sadeeq bil-muraasla*
peninsula *shibh gazeera*
people *naas*
pepper *filfil*
peppermints *niAnaaA*
per: **per night** *fil layla*
perfect *kaamil*
perfume *aiTr*
perhaps *yimkin, rubbama*
perm *tamweeg ish-shaAr*
person *shakhs*; **per person** *in-nafar*
Pharaoh *farAoon*
pharmacy (shop) *saydaleyya*
photocopier *makanit taSweer*

photograph (noun) Soora;
(verb) yiSawwar

photographer muSawwir

phrase book kitaab
TaAbeeraat

piano biyaano

pickpocket nash-shaal

picnic nuz-ha lil-akl

piece Hitta, qiTaa

pillow makhadda,
wisaada

pilot (of aircraft) Tayyaar

pin daaboos

pine (tree) shagarit sonoobar

pineapple ananaas

pink wardee, bamba

pipe (smoking) beeba
(construction, etc)
maasoora, anbooba

pistons basaatim

pizza beetza

place makaan

plant zarA, nabaat

plastic blaastik

plastic bag kees blaastik

plate Taba'

platform raSeef

play (theater) masraHeyya

please (m/f/pl) min
faDlak/-ik/-ukum

plug (electrical) qobs;
(sink) saddaada

plumber sabbaak

pocket gayb

police shurTa, bolees

police officer zaabiT

police report maHDar

police station markaz
ish-shurTa

politics siyyaasa

pond birka

poor fa'eer

pop music mooseeqa gharbee

Popsicle massaasit ays kreem

pork laHm khanzeer

port (harbor) meena

porter (for luggage) shayyaal

possible mumkin

post office mektab il-bareed

postcard kart bostaal

potato baTaaTis

potato chips baTaaTis shibs

poultry id-dawaagin

pound (money) gunayh;
(weight) raTl

powder bodra

prayer mat siggaadit Salaa

prefer yifaDDal

prepared food wagbaat gahza

prescription roshetta

pretty (beautiful) gameel

price siAr

priest qassees

printer makaniT tibaaAa

private khaaSS

problem mushkila; what's the
problem? eh il-mushkila?

profits arbaaH

proposal (business) AarD

public Aaam

public holiday
agaaza rasmeyya

pull yisHab

puncture (tire) agala nayma

purple banafsigee

purse shanTit yad; (change
purse) maHfaza, kees

push yizoh', yidfaA

pyramids il-ahraam(aat)

Q

Qatar qaTar

quality gooda

quay raseef il-meena

question soo'aal

queue (noun) Saff;
(verb) yo'af fis Saff

quick sareeA

quiet haadi

Quran il-qur'aan

R

rabbit arnab

radiator radyateer

radio radyo

radish figl

railcar Aaraba

railroad issikkal-Hadeed

rain maTar

raincoat balTo maTar

raisins zibeeb

range butagaaz

rare (uncommon) naadir;
(steak) sewaa aleel

rat faar

razor blades emwaas

read yi'ra

ready gaahiz, mustaAidd

rear lights fanoos warraanee

receipt wasl

reception istiqbaal

record (music) usTuwaana;
(sporting etc) raqm
qiyaasee

red (m/f) aHmar/Hamra

Red Sea il-baHr il-aHmar

refreshments muraTTibaat

registered mail khiTaab
musaggal

relatives arayeb

relax yistarayyaH

religion deen, deeyaana

remember yiftikir; I don't
remember mish faakir

rent (verb) yi'aggar;
(noun) eegaar

repair (verb) yisallaH;
(noun) tasleeH

report (noun) taqreer

research abHaath

reservation Hagz

reserve yiHgiz

rest (remainder) il-baa'ee;
(relax) istiraaHa

restaurant maTAam

restaurant car Arabeyyit
il-maTAam

restrooms Hammaamaat,
twaalett

return (come back) yirgaA;
(give back) yiraggaA

rice ruzz

rich (wealthy person); ghanee
(heavy food) te'eel

right (correct) SaHeeH;
(direction) yimeen

right away Halaan

ring (to call) yitaSSil
bit-tilifohn; (wedding, etc)
khaatim, dibla

ripe mistewi, naaDig

river nahr

robbery sir'a

road Tareeq, shaareA

roasted fil-furn

rock (stone) Sakhar

roll (bread) Aaysh, khubz

roof satH

room *ghurfa*; (space) *makaan*
room service *khidmit il-ghuraf*
rope *Habl*
roses *ward*
round (circular) *daa'iree*
round-trip *dhahaab w-Aawda*
rowing boat *markib ta'deef*
rubber (material) *kawetsh*
ruby (gemstone)
　yaaqoot aHmar
rug (mat) *siggaada*;
　(blanket) *baTaneyya*
ruins *aTlaal, anqaaD*
ruler (for drawing) *masTara*
run (verb) *yigree*
running *garee*

S

sad *Hazeen*
safe *ma'moon*
safety pin *dabboos amaan*
sailing boat *markib shiraaAee*
salad *salaTa*
sale (at reduced prices)
　okazyon
sales (company) *mubeeAaat*
salmon *salamohn*
salt *malH*
same: the same dress *nafs
　il-fustaan*; the same people
　nafs il-ashkhaas; same again
　kamaan waaHid
sand *raml*
sand dunes *kuthbaan*
sandals *Sandal*
sandwich *sandawitsh*
sanitary napkins *fowaT
　SeHHeyya*
Saturday (yohm) *is-sabt*
sauce *SalSa*
saucepan *Halla*
Saudi Arabia *is-saAoodeeya*
sauna *sohna*
sausage *sugu'*
say *yi'ool*; what did you say?
　ult eh?; how do you say ...?
　izzay ti'ool ...?
scarf *kofeyya, wishaaH*;
　(Islamic headscarf) *Higaab*
schedule *gadwal*
school *madrasa*
science (subject of study)
　il-Auloom

scissors *ma'aSS*
scorpion *Aqrab*
Scotland *iskotlanda*
Scottish *iskotlandee*
screen (computer) *shaasha*
screw *mismaar alawooz*
screwdriver *mufakk*
sea *baHr*
seafood *fawaakih il-baHr*
seat *kursee, maqAad*
seat belt *Hizaam il-maqaAd*
second (of time) *sanya*;
　(in series) *it-taanee*
secretary *sekertayr/a*
see *yishoof*; I can't see
　ena mish shayyif; I see
　(understand) *fahimt*
sell *yibeeA*
send *yibAat*
separate (noun) *munfaSil*;
　(verb) *yifSSil*
separated (man) *munfaSil*;
　(woman) *munfaSila*
September *sebtembir*
serious *khaTeer*
service *khidma*
serviette *fooTa lil-maa'ida*
seven *sabaAa*
sew *yikhayyaT*
shampoo *shamboo*
shave (noun) *Hilaa'a*;
　(verb) *yiHla'*
shaving foam *raghwit Hilaa'a*
shawl *shaal*
she *heyya*
sheep *kharoof*
sheet *milaaya*
shells (sea) *Sadaf*
ship *safeena*
shirt *ameeS*
shoe polish *warneesh il-gazma*
shoe store *maHall gizam*
shoelaces *robaaT il-gazma*
shoes *gazma, gizam*
shopping *tasawwuq*;
　to go shopping *yitsawwaq*
short *uSayyar*
shorts *short*
shoulder *kitf*
shower (bath) *dush*; (rain)
　maTar
shower gel *saayil liddush*
shrimp *gambaree*

shutter (camera) *Haagib
　il-Adasa*; (window) *sheesh*
siblings *ikhwaat*
sick (ill) *mareeD*
side (edge) *Haaffa*
sidelights *anwaar gaanebeyya*
sidewalk *raseef*
sights *maAaalim, manaaZir*
sightseeing *ziyaarit
　il-maAaalim*
sign (verb) *yimDee, yiwaqqaA*;
　(noun) *yafTa*
silk *Hareer*
silver (color) *faDDee*;
　(metal) *faDDa*
simple *baseeT*
sing *yighannee*
single (one) *waaHid*;
　(unmarried) *Aazib*
single room *ghurfa li-shakhS*
sink (noun) *HohD*
sister *ukht*
sitting room *ghurfit guloos*
six *sitta*
size *ma'aas*
skin cleanser *munaZZif
　lil-bashra*
skirt *jeeba, tannoora*
sky *samaa*
sleep (noun) *nohm*; (verb)
　yinaam; to go to
　sleep *yinaam*
sleeping pill *Huboob
　munawwima*
sleeve *komm*
slippers *shibshib*
slow *baTee'*
small *Sughayyar*
smell (noun) *reeyHa*; (verb:
　transitive) *yishimm*
smile (noun) *ibtisaama*;
　(verb) *yibtisim*
smoke (noun) *dukhaan*;
　(verb) *yidakh-khan*
smoking *tadkheen*; non-
　smoking *doon tadkheen*
snack *wagba khafeefa*
snow *galeed*
so: so good! *kwayyis giddan!*
soaking solution (for contact
　lenses); *maHlool lil-Adasaat
　il-laaSiqa*
soap *Saboon*

soccer *koorat il-qadam;*
(ball) *koora*

socks *shawaarib, gawaarib*

soda water *Soda*

sofa *kanaba*

Somalia *is-Somaal*

somebody *Hadd*

something *Haaga*

sometimes *aHyaanan, saaAaat*

son *ibn*

song *ughniya*

sorry! *aasif!;* I'm sorry *ena aasif*

soup *shorba*

south *ganoob*

South Africa *ganoob ifriqya*

South African (man) *ganoob ifriqee;* (woman) *ganoob ifriqeyya;* (adj) *ganoob ifriqee*

souvenir *tizkaar*

spade (shovel) *garoof;*
(cards) *il-bastohnee*

spares *qiTaA ghiyaar*

spark plugs *boojeehaat*

speak (oneself) *yitkallim;*
speak to (someone else) *yikallim;* do you speak ...? *bititkallim(ee) ...?;* I don't speak ... *maa batkallimsh ...*

speed *surAa*

speed limit *Hadd is-surAa*

speedometer *Aaddaad is-surAa*

Sphinx *abul-hohl*

spider *Ankaboot*

spinach *sabaanikh*

spoon *ma'Ala'a*

sports *riyaaDa*

sports ground *naadee riyaaDee*

spring (mechanical) *sosta;*
(season) *ir-rabeeA*

sprinkler *rash-shaash*

square (town) *meedaan*

stadium *istaad*

stairs *sillim*

stamp *TaabiA bareed;*
stamps *TawaabiA bareed*

stapler *dabbaasa*

star *nigma*

start (verb: intransitive) *yibtidee*

station *maHaTTa*

statue *timsaal*

steak *bofteek*

steal *yisra';* it's been stolen *etsara'*

steering wheel *Agalit il-qiyaada*

stewardess *muDeefa*

sting (noun) *ladgha;*
(verb) *yildogh*

stockings *gawaarib Hareemee*

stomach *baTn, maAida*

stomachache *maghaS*

stop (verb) (transitive) *yu'uf;*
(intransitive) *yitwa'af;* (bus stop) *maHaTTit otobeeS;*
stop! *qif!*

store *maHall, dukkaan*

storm *AaaSifa*

straight ahead *Aala Tool*

strawberry *faraawla*

street *shaareA*

string (cord) *doobaara;*
(guitar etc) *watar*

stroller *ArabeyyiT aTfaal*

student *Taalib*

stupid *ghabee*

suburbs *DawaaHee*

Sudan *is-soodaan*

sugar *sukkar*

suit (noun) *badla;* (verb) *yinaasib;* that suits me *dah yinaasibnee*

suitcase *shanTa*

sun *shams*

sunbathe *Hammaam shams*

sunburn *Har'it shams*

Sunday (yohm) *il-Had*

sunglasses *naDaarit shams*

sunny *moshmis*

sunstroke *Darbit shams*

suntan *samaar*

suntan lotion *kereem ish-shams*

supermarket *subermarkit*

supplement *guz' iDaafee*

sure *akeed*

surname *ism il Aayla*

sweat (noun) *Araq;*
(verb) *yiAra'*

sweet (not sour) *Hilw*

swelling *waram*

swim *yisbaH*

swimmer *sabbaaH*

swimming *is-sibaaHa*

swimsuit *mayoh*

swimming pool *Hammaam sibaaHa*

switch (light, etc) *moftaaH*

Switzerland *sweesra*

synagogue *maAbad il-yahood*

Syria *suriya*

syrup (medicinal) *dawa saayil*

T

table *maa'ida, tarabayza*

tablets *Huboob*

take *yakhud*

taking (m/f/pl) *aakhid/ aakhda/aakhdeen*

talcum powder *boodrit talk*

talk (verb) *yitkallim*

tall *Taweel*

taxi *taaksi*

taxi stand *mawqaf taaksi*

tea *shaay*

teacher *mudarris*

telephone (noun) *tilifohn;*
(verb) *yitaSSil bit-tilifohn*

telephone call *mukalma tilifohneyya*

telephone number *nimrit it-tilifohn*

television *tileefizyon*

teller *Sarraaf*

temperature *Haraara*

ten *Aashra*

tent *khayma*

tent peg *wattad il-khayma*

tent pole *Aamood naSb il-khayma*

terminal (airport, etc) *Saala*

tests (medical) *taHaaleel*

thank (verb) *yushkur;* thank you/thanks *shukran;* thank you very much *shukran gazeelan*

that: that cup *il-fingaan dah;*
that man *il-raagil dah;* that woman *is-sitt dee;* what's that? *eh dah?;* I think that ... *aAtaqid an ...*

theater *masraH;* operating theater *ghurfit il-Aamaliyyat*

their ...-*hum;* their room *ghurfithum;* their books *kutubhum;* it's theirs *dah bitaaAhum*

them: it's for them *dah Aalashaan-hum*
there *hinaak*; **there is/are ...** *feeh ...*; **there isn't/aren't ...** *ma feesh ...*
these: these things *il-Haagaat dool*; **these men** *ir-riggaala dool*; **these are mine** *dool bitooAee*
they *humma*
thick *sameek*
thief *Haraamee*
thin *rufayyaA*
think: I think so *aAtaqid*; **I'll think about it** *Hafakker fil-mawDooA*
third *it-taalit*
thirsty: I'm thirsty *ena ATshaan*
this *dah/dee*; **this cup** *il-fingaan dah*; **this man** *il-raagil dah*; **this woman** *is-sitt dee*; **what's this?** *eh dah?*
those: those things *il-Haagaat dool*; **those men** *ir-riggaala dool*; **those are mine** *dool bitooAee*
thousand *elf*
three *talaata*
throat *zawr*
throat pastilles *baasteeliya liz-zawr*
through *khilaal*
thumbtack *dabboos rasm*
thunderstorm *Aasifa raAdeeya*
Thursday *(yohm) il-khamees*
ticket *tazkara*
ticket office *shibbaak tazaakir*
tie (noun) *kravatta*; (verb) *yurbuT*
tights *gawrab Hareemee*
time *wa't, saaAa*; **what time is it?** *is-saaAa kaam?*
timetable *gadwal mawaAeed*
tip (money) *ba'sheesh*; (end) *Tarf*
tire *kawitsh, iTaar*
tired *taAbaan*; **I feel tired** *ashAur bi-taAb*
tissues *manadeel wara'*
to *li*; **quarter to two** *itnayn illa rubA*
toast *tost*
tobacco *dukh-khaan*

today *innahaarda, al-yohm*
together *maAan*
toilet paper *wara' twaalett*
tomato *TamaaTim*
tomato juice *Aaseer TamaaTim*
tomorrow *bukra, ghadan*
tongue *lisaan*
tonight *il-layla (dee)*
too (also) *kamaan, ayDan*; (excessive) *giddan, awee*
tooth *sinn*
toothache *alam asnaan*
toothbrush *furshit asnaan*
toothpaste *maAgoon asnaan*
tour *gawla*
tourist *saayeH*
tourist office *mektab is-siyaaHa*
towel *fooTa*
tower *borg*
town *madeena, balad*
toy *liAba*
toy shop *maHall liAab*
tractor *garraar*
trade fair *maArad tugaaree*
traditions *taqaaleed*
traffic *muroor*
traffic jam *azmit muroor*
traffic lights *ishaara, ishaarit il-muroor*
trailer *maqToora*
train *qiTaar*
train station *maHaTTit qiTaar*
trainee *taHt it-tamreen*
translate *yitargim*
trash *zibaala*
trash can *safeeHit zibaala*
travel agency *wikaalit safareeyaat*
tray *Seneyya*
tree *shagara*; **trees** *shagar*
trip *riHla*
truck *looree*
trunk (car) *shanTa*
try (test) *yigarrab*; (make an effort) *yiHaawil*
Tuesday *(yohm) it-talaat*
Tunisia *toonis*
tunnel *nafa'*
Turkey *turkeya*
turn: turn left/right *khud shimaal/yimeen*

turn signal *ishaara*
tweezers *mil'aaT*
two *itnayn*
two weeks *usbooAyn*

U

umbrella *shamseyya*
uncle (paternal) *Amm*; (maternal) *khaal*
under *taHt*
underground *taHt il-arD*
underpants *kalsoon*
understand *yifham*; **I don't understand** *mish faahim*
underwear *malaabis daakhileyya*
university *gamAa*
unmarried *Aaazib*
until *leHadd, leghaayit*
unusual *ghayr Aadee*
up *foh'*
urgent *mistaAgil*
us: it's for us *dah Aalashaan-na*
use (noun) *fayda*; (verb) *yistakhdim, yistaAmil*
useful *mufeed*
useless *ghayr mufeed*
usual *Aadee*
usually *Aadatan*

V

vacant (rooms) *(ghuraf) faDya*
vacation *agaaza, AuTla*
vacuum cleaner *maknasa kahrabaa'eyya*
vacuum flask *tormos*
valley *waadee*
valve *Simaam*
vanilla *fanelia*
vase *vaaza*
veal *bitello*
vegetables *khuDaar*
vegetarian *nabaatee*
vehicle *sayyaara*
very *giddan, awee*
view *manZar*
viewfinder *muHaddid il-manZar*
villa *filla*
village *qarya*
vinegar *khall*
violin *kammaan*

visa *veeza*

visit (noun) *ziyaara*;
(verb) *yizoor*

visiting hours *mawaaAeed
iz-ziyaara*

visitor *zaayir*;
(tourist) *saayiH*

voice *soht*

voicemail *risaala sohteyya*

W

wait *yistana, yantaZir*;
wait! *istanna!*

waiter *garson*;
waiter! *ya garson!*

waiting room *ghurfit il-intizaar*

Wales *waylz*

walk (noun) *mashyuh*;
(verb) *yimshee*; to go
for a walk *yitmashsha*

wall *heyTa*

wallet *maHfaZa*

want (m/f/pl) *Aawiz/
Aawza/Aawzeen*

war *Harb*

ward *Aanbar*

wardrobe *doolaab*

warm *daafi*

was: I was *ena kunt*; he was
huwa kaan; she was *heyya
kaanit*; it was *kaan*

washing powder *mas-Hooq
ghaseel*

washing-up liquid *saa'il
ghaseel is-suHoon*

watch (noun) *saaAa*;
(verb) *yoraa'ib*

water (noun) *mayya*;
(verb) *yis'ee*

water buffalo *gaamoos*

waterfall *shallaal*

waterpipe (for smoking)
sheesha

wave (noun) *mohga*;
(verb) *yishaawir*

we *iHna*

weather *ig-gaw*

web site *mawqiA Ennit*

wedding *faraH, zafaaf*;
wedding anniversary
Aeed zawaag

Wednesday (yohm) *il-arbaA*

week *usbooA*

welcome *marHaban*; you're
welcome; (don't mention it)
il-Afw

Welsh *min waylz*

were: we were *kunna*; you
were (m/f/pl) *kunt/kuntee/
kuntoo*; they were *kaanoo*

west *gharb*

wet *mablool*

what? *eh?*

wheel *Aagala*

wheelchair *kursee lil-
muqAadeen*

when? *imta?*

where? *fayn?*

which? *ayy(a)?*

white (m/f) *abyaD/bayDa*

who? *meen?*

why? *leh?*

wide *AreeD*

Wi-Fi code *muftaaH lil-wifi*

wife *zohga*

wind *reeH*

window *shibbaak*

windshield *barabreez*

wine *nibeet*

wine list *qaa'emit
in-nibeet*

wing *ginaaH*

with *maAa, bi-*

without *bidoon*

witness *shaahid*

woman *sitt, sayyida*

women's restroom *twaalett
lis-sayyidaat*

wood *khashab*

wool *Soof*

word *kilma*

work (noun) *shughl*;
(verb) *yishtaghil*

working (operative)
shagh-ghaal

world *Aalam*

worry beads *sibHa*

worse (than) *aw-Hash (min)*

wrapping paper *wara' taghleef*

wrench *muftaaH Sawaameel*

wrist *miASam*

write *yiktib*

writing paper *wara' lil-kitaaba*

wrong *khaTa', ghalaT*; wrong
number *in-nimra ghalaT*

X, Y, Z

x-ray *Soorit il-ashiAa*

yacht *yakht*

year *sana*

yellow (m/f) *aSfar/Safra*

Yemen: South Yemen *il-yaman
il-ganoobee*; North Yemen
il-yaman ish-shamaalee

yes *aywah, naAm*

yesterday *imbaariH, ams*

yet *lighaayit dilwa'tee*;
not yet *lissa*

yogurt *zibaadee*

you (m/f/pl) *enta/enti/entum*;
this is for you *dah
Alashaanak (m), dah
Alashaanik (f), dah
Alashaankum (pl)*; with you
*maAaak (m), maAaaki (f),
maAaakum (pl)*

young *Sughayyar (fi sinn)*

your (m/f/pl) *...-ak/-ik/-kum*;
your book (m/f/pl) *kitaabak/
kitaabik/kitaabkum*

yours: is this yours? (m/f/pl)
*dah bitaaAak/bitaaAik/
bitaaAkum?*

youth hostel *bayt ish-shabaab*

zip *sosta*

zoo *Hadeeqit il-Hayawanaat*

THE ARABIC SCRIPT

Introduction

To those accustomed to the Latin alphabet, the Arabic script has an exotic appearance. Right-to-left writing and ornate calligraphic strokes add to the impression of mystery and impenetrability.

However, in spite of first appearances, Arabic script is fundamentally simple and logical. As with any new script, it takes time and practice to be able to read it fluently, but it is not difficult to understand the basic principles nor to learn how to decipher simple words.

The main features of the Arabic script are:

• The direction of writing is from right to left—the opposite direction to most other scripts, including languages such as English that use the Latin alphabet.
• The 28 letters of the alphabet are in most cases joined to each other within a word.
• There are no capital letters.
• Short vowel sounds are not represented in the main Arabic script. These can be written as marks above and below the script but they are usually omitted in modern Arabic.

Letter shapes

Eighteen of the 28 Arabic letters (see pp.155–56) are the same shape as one or more other letters and are only distinguished by dots above or below them.

You can see the similarity between the following groups or pairs of letters:

ب *(b)*   ت *(t)*   ث *(th/t)*

ج *(j/g)*   ح *(H)*   خ *(kh)*

د *(d)*   ذ *(z/d)*

ر (r)   ز (z)

س (s)   ش (sh)

ص (s)   ض (D)

ط (T)   ظ (z/D)

ع (A)   غ (gh)

The dots that distinguish one letter from another that is the same shape are part of the basic script and are not optional like the vowel markings (see Additional marks, p.157).

The remaining ten letters of the Arabic alphabet each have a unique shape, but some look like other letters when they are joined to other letters within a word (see pp.154-56).

ا (alif)   ف (f)

ق (q/')   ك (k)

ل (l)   م (m)

ن (n)   ه (h)

و (w/oo)   ي (y/ee)

Note: The letter **alif** is the first letter of the Arabic alphabet and the only one that can be pronounced in a range of different ways. It can represent any short vowel or the longer **aa** sound.

Joining letters

Arabic writing is cursive, or "joined up," and is only rarely written as separate letters - for example, in a crossword.

All 28 letters can be joined to the letter before them in a word, and all but six can be joined to the letter after them. The shape of a letter changes when it is joined to others, but it still retains enough features to make it recognizable.

In general, when an Arabic letter is joined to the letter after it (to the left), it loses any left-hand tail or flourish it has when on its own. It still, however, keeps any dots above or below it, to distinguish it from other letters of the same shape. Look at the examples below, read from right to left, starting at top right:

م + ص + ر = مصر   ف + ج + ر = فجر

ط + ب + ق = طبق   ع + ن + د = عند

س + ب + ت = سبت   ف + ي + ه = فيه

Note how the shapes of the letters ع (**A**), غ (**gh**), ك (**k**), and ه (**h**) change when they are joined to another letter.

م + ع = مع   س + ك + ر = سكر

ك + ل = كل   م + غ + ر = مغر

ه + ي = هي   ن + ه + ر = نهر

The six letters - ا (**alif**), د (**d**), ذ (**dh/z**), ر (**r**), ز (**z**), and و (**w/oo**) - that are never joined to any letter after them, always have a space between them and the next letter:

ا + ب = اب   ز + و + ج = زوج

د + ا + ر = دار   ا + ن + ت = انت

The Arabic alphabet

The table below shows all the letters in Arabic alphabetical order. You can see how their shapes change depending on whether they are separate from any other letter, or the first, middle letter, or last letter in a word.

Separated	First	Middle	Last
ا (see p.153)	ا	ـل	ـل
ب (b)	بـ	ـبـ	ـب
ت (t)	تـ	ـتـ	ـت
ث (th/t)	ثـ	ـثـ	ـث
ج (j/g)	جـ	ـجـ	ـج
ح (H)	حـ	ـحـ	ـح
خ (kh)	خـ	ـخـ	ـخ
د (d)	د	ـد	ـد
ذ (dh/z)	ذ	ـذ	ـذ
ر (r)	ر	ـر	ـر
ز (z)	ز	ـز	ـز
س (s)	سـ	ـسـ	ـس
ش (sh)	شـ	ـشـ	ـش
ص (s)	صـ	ـصـ	ـص
ض (D)	ضـ	ـضـ	ـض
ط (T)	ط	ـط	ـط
ظ (z/D)	ظ	ـظـ	ـظ

Separated	First	Middle	Last
ع (A)	عـ	ـعـ	ـع
غ (gh)	غـ	ـغـ	ـغ
ف (f)	فـ	ـفـ	ـف
ق (q/')	قـ	ـقـ	ـق
ك (k)	كـ	ـكـ	ـك
ل (l)	لـ	ـلـ	ـل
م (m)	مـ	ـمـ	ـم
ن (n)	نـ	ـنـ	ـن
ه (h)	هـ	ـهـ	ـه
و (w/oo)	و	ـو	ـو
ي (y/ee)	يـ	ـيـ	ـي

Hamza

The **hamza** is a small sign that can appear above or below other letters (`ə ʃ ¬æ ¿æ`), or by itself (µ). The **hamza** represents a glottal stop (as in *butter* said as "*bu'er*"), but is not strongly pronounced in spoken Arabic. It can sometimes be heard as a small pause in the middle of a word, similar to the spoken pronunciation of ì (q/').

أب (*ab*/father)

مائدة (*maa'ida*/table)

Feminine ending

There is a special character that indicates a feminine ending: ة. This is called **taa maboota** ("tied-up T") and looks like a cross between the letters ™ (**h**) and H (**t**). It is only ever used at the end of a word and is generally pronounced **a**, but the pronunciation changes to **t** (or sometimes **it**) when an ending is added, or when the word is used in a compound phrase:

تذكرة (tazkara/ticket)

تذكرتين (tazkartayn/two tickets)

زوجة (zohga/wife)

زوجتي (zohgtee/my wife)

زوجة أمير (zohgit ameer/Amir's wife)

Additional marks

Short vowels and double letters are indicated by marks above and (in one case) below the script:

ـَ = a/e   ـُ = u/o   ـِ = i   ـّ = double letter

مَحَطّة (манатта/station)

بُرج (borg/tower)

مَسجِد (masgid/mosque)

Most modern written Arabic does not show these marks (it is assumed that the reader is familiar with the pronunciation), and this can make reading the script challenging for learners. But most beginners find that reading Arabic script without vowel marks becomes easier with practice, as the patterns of the Arabic language become more familiar. Look back at some of the words and phrases in this book and see if you can work out the Arabic script using the alphabet table on pp.155-56 and the pronunciation guide given in the lessons.

USEFUL SIGNS

Here are some useful signs you may see around you in the Arabic-speaking world.

dukhool
Entrance

khuroog
Exit

dawraat miyaah
Restrooms

rigaal
Men

sayyidaat
Women

khaтar
Danger

ممنوع التدخي

mamnooᴀ it-tadkheen
No smoking

ممنوع الدخو

mamnooᴀ id-dukhool
Do not enter

mustashfa
Hospital

bank
Bank

markaz ish-shurⲦa
Police station

mektab il-bareed
Post office

محطة القطا

maⲎaⲦⲦit il-qitaar
Train station

مطا

maⲦaar
Airport

Acknowledgments

The publisher would like to thank the following for their help in the preparation of this book: Abu Zaad Restaurant, Shepherd's Bush; Magnet Showroom, Enfield, London; MyHotel, London; Peppermint Green Hairdressers, London; Capel Manor College; The Savoy Hotel, Sharm El Sheikh; Richard Simmons; Jane Gibbon and Max.

The publisher would also like to thank the following people who appear as models: Ahmed Mahmoud Mubarak; Heidi Kirolos; Mahitab El A'war; Mai Kholief; Mahmoud El Beleidy; Haneen El-Beih; Amina Mansour; Abdelrahman Ayman Helry; Mena Talla Hassan El Menabawy; Hayat Kamil; Pia Noor; Neelpa Odedra; Adam Brackenbury; Silke Spingies; Mini Vhra; Adam Walker; Martha Evatt; Mehdi Khandan; Michael Duffy; Sue Alniab; Jason Carnegie; Abdullah Akhazzan; Mahmoud Gafaar.

Language content for Dorling Kindersley by **g-and-w publishing**
Managed by **Jane Wightwick**
Editing and additional input: **Cathy Gaulter-Carter, Teresa Cervera, Leila Gaafar**

Additional editorial assistance: **Lynn Bresler**
Picture research: **Schermuly Design Co.**

Picture credits

Key: *a-above; b-below/bottom; c-center; f-far; l-left; r-right; t-top*

123RF.com: *luzitanija 108b;* **Alamy Images:** *82fcrb, 85tc, 103cla, 107bc, 115cla, 115tl; Bartomeu Amengual 69clb, 76crb; Arcaid 65bl, 66ca; Comstock Images 30fbr; concepts of stock 13cr; Gary Cook 50-51c; Deco Images 53ftl; Julius Fekete 48c, 56ca; Grapheast 12, 14crb, 17c, 28crb; Nick Hanna 73tl; Andrew Holt 11tl; D. Hurst 103tl; Image Source Pink 61cl; imagebroker 40ca, 55cla, 56ftr; ImageState Royalty Free 95bl; Ingram Publishing (Superstock Limited) 58cra, 67ca; Israel Images 10c, 17cb; James Dawson / Image Farm Inc. 53cla; John Foxx 13cra, 17ca; Jupiter Images/Creatas 13crb; Jupiterimages/ Brand 54cr; Jupiterimages/ Brand X 58crb, 85c, 91t; Jupiterimages/ Comstock Images 84-85c; christian kober 118-119c; Andrew Linscott 98-99c; Bill Lyons 23clb; Gail Mooney-Kelly 49fbl, 56cla; Panacea Pictures 44fbr; PCL 49clb, 56fcla; Helene Rogers 73cla, 94cr; Rubber Ball 13br; jackson smith 54br; Petr Svarc 45fbl; Think Stock 30br; Thinkstock LLC 55tl; THP Travel 103ftl; Trip 114cr; Ultimate Group, LLC 120br, 124cb; wildphotos.com 83tl;* **Corbis:** *Tibor Bognar 48-49c;* **Dreamstime.com:** *Slobodan Mračina 15cl; Slobodan Mračina 15cb; Slobodan Mračina 36cra;* **Getty Images:** *Datacraft 65cr; Insy Shah 33cr; Rob Melnychuk 80-81c;* **Ingram Image Library:** *22fbr, 61clb, 65ftr, 67bc, 74-75cb, 82cr, 91clb, 97cla, 122clb, 124bc; Ingram Image Library 13tl, 14cr, 15cra, 29bl, 29clb;* **iStockphoto.com:** *nicolas_ 35tl, 37ca; alvarez 82tr; Philippa Banks 29cl; vera bogaerts 59tl, 103bc; Sam Heaton 60bl; Mark Kostich 82cra; Sean Locke 78br, 86br; Nicolas Loran 35tl, 37ca; Vassiliki Palamari 40br; Curt Pickens 99cb;* **Photolibrary:** *122-123c;* **Renault (UK):** *40c, 46cr, 56b;* **Savoy/Sharm el Sheikh:** *5tl, 60cr, 6667bc;* **Shutterstock:** *93cla, 97bc; Anyka 119tl; Yuri Arcurs 73cl; Avesun 84fbl; Carme Balcells 95clb; vera bogaerts 65clb; WH Chow 43cra; Jim Cox 98fbl; Creatista 113tl, 116ca; Deklofenak 58cr, 67tc; Ersler Dmitry 99bc, 107cl; Tom Grundy 61tl, 66cra; Ramzi Hachicho 4bl, 104br; Amy Nichole Harris 74bc; Igor_S 85crb; Tischenko Irina 109tl, 116cb; André Klaassen 65tl; Romeo Koitmäe 121tl; Vladimir Korostyshevskiy 49cla; L F File 104tc, 125cla; Maceofoto 73ftl; Pavle Marjanovic 40cr, 46bc; Rob Marmion 111cl; Holger Mette 41fbl; Nastiakru 36cr; Zsolt Nyulaszi 94br; Nick Poling 120-121c, 124crb; RexRover 112bl; spe 68fbl; Vadym Stetsenko 5tr, 64crb; Vibrant Image Studio 65cra; Lisa F. Young 110cr.*

All other images © **Dorling Kindersley**
For further information see: **www.dkimages.com**